Routledge Revivals

The Power of the Prime Minister

Originally published in 1968, the theme of this book is the decline of the influence of the House of Commons in general and the rise in particular in the power of the Prime Minister. The author looks behind the myths of how our constitution operates to describe what was actually happening in practice in the 2nd half of the 20th Century. The book highlights the way in which the Commons was filing to check and control the executive. It also makes valuable suggestions (which have since been adopted) to set up specialist committees, to consider the principal political issues of the day and how the House of Lords might be reformed.

The Power of the Prime Minister

Humphry Berkeley

Routledge
Taylor & Francis Group

First published in 1968 by George Allen & Unwin Ltd.

This edition first published in 2024 by Routledge
4 Park Square, Milton Park, Abingdon, Oxon, OX14 4RN
and by Routledge
605 Third Avenue, New York, NY 10158.

Routledge is an imprint of the Taylor & Francis Group, an informa business

ISBN 13: 978-1-032-86345-0 (hbk)
ISBN 13: 978-1-003-52712-1 (ebk)
ISBN 13: 978-1-032-86347-4 (pbk)
Book DOI 10.4324/9781003527121

THE POWER
OF THE
PRIME MINISTER

HUMPHRY BERKELEY

FOREWORD BY
NORMAN ST JOHN-STEVAS, MP

London
GEORGE ALLEN AND UNWIN LTD
RUSKIN HOUSE MUSEUM STREET

PRINTED IN GREAT BRITAIN
in 12 *on* 13 *point Fournier*
BY UNWIN BROTHERS LTD
WOKING AND LONDON
(9994 B)

FOREWORD

BY NORMAN ST JOHN-STEVAS, MP

When Mr Humphry Berkeley asked me to write an introduction to his book, I was both flattered and dismayed; flattered that it should be thought that I could add anything worthwhile to his reflections, dismayed that advancing years have apparently opened a new rôle for me. It seems to me not so very long ago that A. P. Herbert was kind enough to write a foreword to *my* first book. Yet my dominant feeling is one of pleasure in being able to commend a book of a former colleague in parliament for whom I have both admiration and esteem. Mr Humphry Berkeley is not only a man of great political ability but what is even rarer of outstanding political courage. As he tells us himself in the text, he voted against his own party six times on matters of principle in the seven years he was in parliament. Though I feel ashamed to admit it, since I have gathered some slight reputation for independent thought, I have never voted against the party so much as once! Men of courage and independence are rare in our contemporary parliament and although Westminster misses few of them, the House of Commons does miss the author of this book. It is a less stimulating place without *him*. I hope that it will not be long before he is back at Westminster—a feeling which I believe is shared by many, not all of whom would necessarily agree with his views.

The theme of this book is the decline of the influence of the House of Commons in general and the rise in particular of the power of the Prime Minister. Mr Berkeley, like Walter Bagehot before him, is looking behind the myths of how our constitution operates, to describe what is actually happening in practice. We are heading, he believes—indeed we may have it already—towards a presidential system of government moderated only

7

by the occasional plebiscites of the electorate. There is much that is true in the author's analysis of the way in which the Commons today is failing to check and control the executive. The traditional parliamentary means of control, question time and the use of adjournment debates are perfunctory and inadequate. When legislation is drafted all affected interests are normally consulted but Memebers of Parliament are then faced with a *fait accompli;* they come on the scene too late to exercise effective influence. Government supporters are inhibited by the need to keep the administration in office from pressing their views to a division while Opposition members can always be voted down. Backed by the resources of a well equipped and able civil service, a minister of reasonable ability is for most of the time invulnerable.

While much of this is true, I think Mr Berkeley's picture of parliamentary obsolescence and futility does need to be balanced by other considerations. Parliamentary government still has its uses, and I would single out two in particular. First, it brings to the service of the state what Bagehot called 'an unrivalled average of continued ability'. If in normal conditions it excludes from office the original geniuses, the men of farseeing minds and dominating wills, it also keeps out the fools. Sheer incompetence cannot survive for long the daily glare of the dispatch box: it has to be dismissed. Parliamentary government gives us an unbroken series of capable ministers by a kind of natural selection. A parliamentary statesman only emerges after long years of trial and after winnowing in the 'face to face' encounters of speech and action which constitute the essence of parliamentary life. Even the member who never achieves office can influence the course of public events, although that influence is necessarily diffuse and cumulative. Personality still counts in the Commons and in the nation. We are, after all, not governed by computers or steam engines but by men.

Second, parliamentary government prevents corruption and checks, if it does not exclude, injustice. The scope for corruption in a civil service subject to parliamentary scrutiny through the application of the doctrine of ministerial responsibility is extremely limited. In authoritarian states quite the reverse is true as has been shown by Napoleon III's France or Mussolini's Italy. We take the purity and integrity of those in our civil service and public life so much for granted that we fail to realise what a rarity it is in the history of civilisation. As to injustice, its excesses are being continually checked not only by the actual interventions of wrathful and zealous M.P.s but by ministerial knowledge that such initiatives may at any time be taken. Every minister knows that he will have to answer for his actions in the public forum of the House of Commons and this knowledge is an effective deterrent against arbitrary action and tyranny. Had the parliamentary commissioner been given adequate powers, he would have been able greatly to assist members' efforts to right individual injustices.

Nevertheless, that having been said, all is not well with the Commons and I think Mr Berkeley's suggestion for the setting up of specialist committees, with a semi-permanent membership, to consider the principal political issues of the day and summon ministers and civil servants before them, an excellent one. In legislative matters they could bring their influence to bear before departmental policies had hardened and if (as he suggests) members also sat on the legislative committees considering bills after drafting, their influence could be greatly increased. The individual member would be further strengthened if adequate research and secretarial facilities were made available. Every member should have a full time secretary and a full time research assistant paid out of public funds.

The existence of these pre-legislative committees would strengthen the position of the individual member in the most practical way possible by giving him something important to do. The lack of an effective rôle for back-bench members whether they be on the government or opposition side of the House is in my view the principal reason for their decline in public esteem. At present their principal function is to vote automatically at party behest for or against the government—a rôle inevitable in a system of mass democracy which could not work without a fairly disciplined party structure. It is futile to wring one's hands over the passing of the independence of members which was so marked in the 'classic' period of parliamentary government of mid-Victorian times, since this was a by-product of a limited suffrage. Party discipline is the unavoidable corrollary of universal suffrage and there can be no going back on that. A frontal assault on the party system is simply not practical, but by giving members new scope some of its worst effects could be circumvented. The adoption of the alternative vote, as suggested by Mr Berkeley, would also greatly strengthen the independent member by enabling him to appeal, if necessary, from the small caucus of party workers in the constituencies to party supporters in the constituency as a whole. At present if the member loses the support of the caucus it is equivalent to losing his seat, since party supporters are not prepared to risk letting in a member of the opposite party by splitting their vote. An alternative voting system would enable them to express their personal preferences without risking such a consequence. I fear however that it is unlikely to be adopted in practice since it would greatly strengthen the chances of a third party, such as the Liberals. Whichever of the present major parties is in office would hardly countenance this, unless driven to make an electoral deal by a position in the House of Commons where the third party held the balance of power.

Mr Berkeley also has some radical proposals for directly checking the power of the Prime Minister. He favours taking away his power of dissolving the chamber—parliament would be elected for a fixed term of five years—and the imposition of a further limitation on the period in which any individual could hold that office of eight years. Here I am afraid I cannot go along with him. It would I believe introduce a rigidity in the constitution which would be highly undesirable. Mr Berkeley points to the American parallels to buttress his arguments, but even under that system this sort of check has led more to paralysis of government than to anything else. In any case, however much the powers of the Prime Minister may have increased (and it is possible to under-estimate the influence of the cabinet), there is still an unbridgeable gulf between the Congressional and Parliamentary systems of government since, while the President can govern without Congress, the Prime Minister cannot govern without Parliament. An election which produces an indecisive result can always be remedied by a further dissolution after a short period of time which is what in effect happened in the general elections of 1964 and 1966. To perpetuate a weak government for five years, which would be a very real hazard of Mr Berkeley's system, would I believe be too high a price to pay for clipping the Prime Minister's wings.

Mr Berkeley has not forgotten that we are a bi-cameral legislature and his suggestions for the reform of the Lords are highly relevant now that this has become a live issue once again. He has some wise things to say about the rôle of the Lords as a forum for independent opinion and as a chamber in which industrial, ecclesiastical, professional and other non-party interests could be represented.

In all, this is a timely and valuable book, the fruit of both reflection and experience. Like myself, other readers of this book will agree with some proposals and reject others, but I think everyone will concur that Mr Berkeley has made a worthwhile contribution to our political life by putting his ideas into circulation. This is a book well within the established tradition of Tory radicalism, of which the author is such a distinguished exponent, and as such it deserved a warm welcome.

NORMAN ST JOHN-STEVAS

ACKNOWLEDGEMENTS

I am grateful to Jonathan Sumption for undertaking a considerable amount of research for this book and for his help in drafting two of the Chapters.

James Skinner, David Rogers and Geoffrey Block have read the book in draft and have both made invaluable suggestions for its improvement.

My debt to Colin Harris is of a different order. I have discussed every aspect of the book with him; he helped me to plan its contents; he has undertaken a massive amount of research and drafting. He has carefully read through each chapter in draft. I can truthfully say that without his help the book could not have been written.

November 1st 1967   HUMPHRY BERKELEY

CONTENTS

CHAPTER I

THE POWER OF THE PRIME MINISTER

The speech which made the greatest impact on me during the six and a half years in which I sat in the House of Commons was delivered by the late Aneurin Bevan. The greatest Parliamentarian within my personal experience, Bevan spoke during the debate on the Queen's speech a few days after my election to Parliament in November 1959. He said, 'Therefore I would suggest, in an entirely non-party spirit, . . . that members opposite, especially new members, must realize that there stretches before them endless hours of infinite boredom, almost limitless stretches of arid desert, that will be almost unendurable unless we can put in a few oases ourselves here and there'. I took this to be light-hearted banter at the time, but in my experience it is true. Something is seriously wrong with the Mother of Parliaments.

To define exactly what is wrong is a different matter. Certain facts are obvious. The House of Commons spends hours of Parliamentary time discussing matters of utmost triviality. Great issues are frequently not discussed. A Foreign Affairs debate may be held only twice a year. In twelve hours, four of which are allocated to front bench spokesmen, the House of Commons is expected to discuss matters as far removed from each other as Vietnam, the Middle East, Aden, Europe and contemporary trends in the Cold War. In a debate such as this, probably not more than a quarter of the number of members who wish to speak are actually called. On other occasions the Whips have to bustle around to find enough members to speak on matters of little interest to them and even less to their constituents in order to prevent the debate from collapsing.

The length of speeches—I am sure that this is not just my imagination—has tended to increase. It is comparatively rare now for a speaker to make even a perfunctory reference to the speeches that have gone before: for this reason there is little point in remaining in the Chamber to listen to the rest of the debate after one has been called. Nor does anybody pretend, except on the rarest of occasions, that anything said in debate has any influence on anybody's opinion or any effect on Government action.

I do recall one such occasion in July 1964 when Mr Henry Brooke, then Home Secretary, moved that the Police Pensions (No. 2) Regulations be approved at 10 p.m. after the main debate had concluded. Apparently during the day Members of Parliament had been receiving telegrams of protest from the Police Federation. To the surprise of many the chamber remained full after the 10 p.m. division. It soon became clear that there was considerable opposition to this measure from both sides of the House. The measure provided that the widow of a policeman who died as a result of an attack while attempting to make an arrest would be entitled to a special rate of pension and to a gratuity. Back benchers on both sides of the House held that it was wrong to discriminate between the widows of policemen who had been attacked and the widows of those who had died, for example, through falling from a roof while attempting to arrest a criminal.

Excellent speeches—short, telling, moving and to the point were made from both sides of the House. Sir Spencer Summers aptly referred to the debate as 'one of those rare occasions when back benchers bring an influence to bear on the front bench.' Certainly they were successful, for the Home Secretary was forced to undertake that legislation would be introduced which would widen the scope of the compensation along the lines generally desired. Afterwards, in the lobbies and corridors as members chatted, I recall that we congratulated ourselves on the remarkable way in which the House of Commons can act to prevent the Government of the day from committing injustice. On my way home that night I could not help asking myself if it really was so remarkable that the House of Commons should assert itself in this way once every few years, particularly when it did so only in response to a mass approach from a professional body, in a cause that would cost very little money and when no political principle was at stake.

I felt this particularly because by contrast on the previous evening we had considered the Obscene Publications Bill. An amendment was moved from the Labour benches providing that when a book was proceeded against and the defence wished to ask for expert evidence, the defence should be able to apply for the case to be heard before a jury and not before a single individual. This too was not an issue that could remotely be said to arouse party political controversy, still less to involve political principle. The Solicitor-General rejected the amendment on behalf of the Conservative Government. A division took place at 8.13 p.m. Members who had not listened to a word of the debate poured out of the Members dining room at some risk to their digestive systems, and the amendment was defeated by 124 votes to 81 with only two Conservatives, myself and Mr Ian Gilmour voting in favour of this elementary protection to the accused individual.

These two incidents, happening as they did on successive days, brought home to me at the time the relative impotence of Parliament. In the latter case there is surely a lot to be said in favour of free votes on matters of this kind. It cannot seriously be suggested that Members of Parliament are unable to make up their minds on issues such as this, as is sometimes claimed by the Whips, but if some are unable to do so, would it not be better if their votes went unrecorded?

One trouble is that so many people are mesmerized by the totally false constitutional doctrine that if a Government is defeated, even in Committee on a peripheral matter, it has to resign. When I voted against the Conservative Government in 1961 to establish the right of Mr Anthony Wedgwood Benn to be heard at the Bar of the House of Commons I was solemnly asked by a Government Whip if I really wanted the Government to fall on such an issue. I retorted that if the Government was foolish enough to regard this as a vote of confidence it deserved to fall. Obviously the Government needs to be assured of the support of its back benchers on the major items of its legislative programme; obviously it must be able to rely on a good majority when it calls for a vote of confidence. No responsible party member would think of withholding his vote on frivolous grounds. But is it really necessary for the Whip to be applied indiscriminately on matters great and small and on issues that have no obvious political content.

My six and a half years in Parliament have convinced me that our parliamentary institutions, particularly when the myth is distinguished from the reality, are insufficient by themselves to safeguard our freedom. Indeed the absence of any defined separation of powers between the executive and the legislature has enabled already strong Governments to use Parliament only too easily as an instrument of tyranny. Paradoxically the British have been attempting to export the Westminster parliamentary system and use it as the sole protection of the consent of the governed in Africa and Asia at the very point when it has ceased to provide a similar safeguard at home. Westminster democracy has broken down in Britain not because of unfamiliarity with its processes nor because it was alien to our society and customs. On the contrary, by the nineteenth century, its classic period, it had evolved through six hundred years of trial and error and it evolved quite simply because its participants willed it to work. A hundred years ago Bagehot was able to write 'The characteristic merit of the English Constitution is that its dignified parts are very complicated and somewhat imposing and very old and rather venerable; while its efficient part, at least when in great and critical action, is decidedly simple and rather modern'. The dignified parts were those elements which gave ceremonial stability to the country, namely the Monarchy and the House of Lords. The efficient part was where the power lay—by Bagehot's definition, the House of Commons.

In fact at the time when Bagehot was writing, the House of Commons was already being transformed into one of the dignified parts of the Constitution. It was to be overshadowed temporarily by the Cabinet and this body in turn has been superseded by disguised presidential rule on the part of the Prime Minister, buttressed not by Parliament but by the Civil Service and the Party Machine.

Bagehot was right to describe the efficient secret of the British Constitution as 'the close union, the nearly complete fusion of the executive and legislative powers'. But this is not to say that it is desirable for the executive to have all the powers and the legislature to have none; indeed it was with this danger in mind that the drafters of the American Constitution insisted upon a separation of powers and functions. Nor was it true to say in the nineteenth century that this fusion of powers had become the wholesale take-over on the part of the executive that we witness today.

The twentieth century has seen an immense extension of the administrative powers of government. It has also seen the creation of the modern party machines. Both developments have given power to bodies which are irresponsible in the sense that they are not subject to democratic direction. The former has immensely increased the power of the Civil Service—to quote from the Labour Party evidence to the Fulton Committee, 'Much more difficult to justify is the amount of information which in some departments at least is kept from the Minister. Some of it is planning work which is deliberately concealed from him, either because it might lead him to support policies which the department does not approve of, or even because it is being done in preparation for a future government of a different political colour. It is this secrecy which makes some ministers tools of their departments a good deal of the time.' Oddly enough the strict application of the doctrine of ministerial responsibility which still exists in theory has actually added to the power and invulnerability of the Civil Service. For no minister can nowadays hope to be fully aware of all the acts which are carried out in his name by his Departmental Civil Servants. Yet, to take one example, in the case of Crichel Down in 1954, the Minister accepted responsibility for his civil servants and was expected to resign, even though some of the civil servants involved were transferred. There were also suggestions early in 1967 that Mr Roy Jenkins should resign when the number of prisoners escaping from jail appeared to be unusually high. For the Minister alone to be judged to be accountable to Parliament for actions of which he may have no knowledge (and of which he might disapprove if he had) is another example of the conflict between myth and reality in our constitutional practice, which actually prevents Parliament from carrying out one of its traditional functions of redressing grievance. For under our practice the Civil Servant, who in many cases is actually responsible for decisions, cannot be questioned on them.

The creation of the party machines has seen the emergence of two new political phenomena; the full-time paid party functionary and the local party boss, of whom Alderman Salvidge of Liverpool was perhaps the first. Sir Michael Fraser, the Deputy Chairman of the Conservative Central Office, is perhaps the prototype of the new Party Civil Servant. He was appointed by the leader of the Conservative Party to whom he is personally responsible for the organization of the Conservative Machine and the Conservative Research Department. He has never sat in Parliament, nor held any elective office on the voluntary side of the Conservative Party, nor had experience of commerce or industry. His whole adult career has been that of a paid party servant. His influence is greater than that of any backbench MP and of most members of the Shadow Cabinet. His sphere of authority exceeds that of any General Director of the Conservative Central Office, whose role he has inherited in addition to other functions. His appointment denotes a professionalism and career structure within the Conservative Party organization comparable to that of a large Government Department. There are signs of a growing professionalism in the Labour Party organization as well.

Both these developments have reduced the prestige of Parliament and the status of individual Members of Parliament. To quote Richard Crossman, the present Leader of the House of Commons, in his introduction to Bagehot's *The English Constitution*[1] 'In a period when effective power in all spheres of life, economic social and political is being concentrated in fewer and fewer hands, parliamentary control of the executive has been steadily decreasing without being replaced by any other methods of democratic control'.

The hallmark of an unwritten constitution is unperceived change. I have written this book because after six and a half years in the House of Commons, although never in office, I have seen the interaction of the legislature and the executure at sufficiently close quarters to realize that almost every premise on which my knowledge of constitutional theory was based has turned out to be untrue. Parliament is not in practice sovereign. The Prime Minister is not, and has not been for a very long time, *primus inter pares*. We do not have Cabinet Government. The ancient parliamentary rivalry between the Lords and the Commons has for years been irrelevant. For the issue is not whether the House of Lords should for a few fleeting months defy the elected Chamber, but whether Parliament as a whole can ever act as a curb on the Government. Ministerial accountability to Parliament acts as a shelter for anonymous but increasingly potent civil servants. The party machines, which have increasingly become the personal property of the Party leaders, so far from

[1] London: Fontana Books.

being the instruments of achieving parliamentary dominance (as opposed to parliamentary majorities) have actually brought about the unchecked presidential rule by which Britain is governed today.

I have become convinced that the central defect in our form of government is the excessive power of the Prime Minister. To quote Sir Alec Douglas Home in an interview in *The Observer* a year before he became Prime Minister, 'Every Cabinet Minister is in a sense the Prime Minister's agent—his assistant. There is no question about that. It is the Prime Minister's Cabinet and he is the one person directly responsible to the Queen for what the Cabinet does. If the Cabinet discusses anything it is the Prime Minister who decides what the collective view of the Cabinet is. A Minister's job is to save the Prime Minister all the work he can. But no Minister could make a really important move without consulting the Prime Minister, and if the Prime Minister wants to take a certain step the Cabinet Minister would either have to agree, to argue it out in Cabinet, or resign.'

Supported, like the American President, by a formidable Civil Service and a nationally based party machine, and served by an obedient Cabinet, the Prime Minister does not require the infinite patience which characterizes the President's dealings with Congress. For he is not the inheritor of the intricately delicate separation of powers which the authors of the American constitution devised to prevent Presidential Government from becoming a four-year tyranny.

In this book I trace the historic steps that have been taken, many of them almost imperceptible, which have led to the Prime Minister's present position of impregnability. I make proposals for a readjustment of powers as between Downing Street, Whitehall and Westminster. For if one is to reject government by referendum, as I do, a clearly defined division of powers between Parliament and Government is essential. It is no less important for Parliament to be equipped to fill this much needed role.

In March 1966 I completed nearly seven years in Parliament.

It was of course an incomparable privilege to sit in Parliament with Sir Winston Churchill. I never heard him speak in the Chamber, but his almost daily presence provided a link with a historic past. These years also saw the tragic deaths of Aneurin Bevan and Hugh Gaitskell and the retirement of Harold Macmillan as Prime Minister. These events impoverished the House and made it seem a little smaller and more mundane, rather as a school would be affected by the sudden loss of its finest products. I have witnessed the excitement of great events—the announcement by Mr Macmillan late at night of the signature of the nuclear test ban treaty in Moscow, and the suspense of waiting for the announcement of the voting figures at the conclusion of the Profumo debate. I have seen the dawn break over the Thames after an all night sitting. I have seen the House in crowded uproar, and at times so empty that it called to mind the last flickering moments of a dying man. I have also known the endless hours of infinite boredom about which new members were warned by Aneurin Bevan. The truth of this warning is my predominant impression after my period in Parliament. This convinces me that a radical overhaul of the relationship between the legislature and the executive is urgently required.

CHAPTER II

THE GROWTH OF POWER

'Democracy', wrote Shaw, 'substitutes election by the incompetent many for appointment by the corrupt few.' A broad view of the British Constitution could distinguish three periods in its history, a period of corrupt oligarchy, a period of incompetent democracy, and a brief period in between, during which the Member of Parliament, subject to neither the temptations of corruption nor the pressures of incompetence, lived up to the ideal created for him by the constitutional theorists.

Harold Nicolson, in his biography of George V, has attributed the constitutional development of the last two centuries to a 'historical accident', namely the accession of a German-speaking Hanoverian in 1714. 'Even the halting Latin in which his ministers sought to convey their desires', he continues, 'was spoken with so strong a public school accent that it was to him incomprehensible. He therefore ceased to preside at the meetings of the Cabinet, and his place as chairman was taken by the senior minister, who gradually became known as the "prime minister".' It can be pointed out that only fifteen years elapsed before Walpole became the 'first prime minister'.

The novelty of this can be exaggerated. There had often been chief ministers in English history before 1714, but they had always depended on the favour of the Crown. After the Restoration there were still many areas in which the King could act without Parliament and one of them was the choice of ministers, who therefore continued to be regarded as 'the King's men'.

Moreover, it was not until the eighteenth century that the Crown delegated its power of supervising ministers. This meant that neither Clarendon nor Godolphin were Prime Ministers in the accepted sense of the term. The position of both rested on their ability to persuade the King to accept their point of view. Clarendon himself did not seek any greater power and believed that people should be ruled by an absolute monarch rather than by a 'lawful monarch who rules through a Prime Minister'. Anne always considered her ministers to be her servants, but during her reign the movement towards Cabinet government accelerated very considerably. Not only did the Cabinet begin to meet frequently but, despite Anne's endeavours to free herself from 'party tyranny', it came to represent only the dominant political faction: the refusal of the Whigs to serve in the die-hard Tory ministry of 1710 was a landmark in the history of Cabinet government. The final achievement of Cabinet government can be dated to 1729, when Townshend's resignation left Walpole to unite in one man, for the first time in English history, the confidence of the Crown and the support of Parliament: 'When I speak here as being a minister', he told the House of Commons, 'I speak as possessing my powers from his majesty but as being answerable to this house for the exercise of these powers.' His power, which was already little short of absolute, was matched only by his ambition, which led him to exclude all others from effective power. His fall in 1742 can be construed as the revenge of excluded politicians, but the important fact was that it was accomplished through Parliament. It was essentially this balance of political power which was bequeathed to the nineteenth century.

The storm of invective and abuse which greeted the constitutional innovation of a first minister basing his power on parliamentary support at the time is illuminating in view of the developments of the last hundred years. 'A Prime Minister', complained a number of peers in 1731, 'is an officer unknown to the law of Britain, inconsistent with the constitution of this country, and destructive of liberty in any government what-soever'. The indignation which faced Lord North after the loss of the American colonies obliged him openly to justify in theory the powers which his predecessors had long exercised in practice. 'In critical times', he said, 'it is necessary that there should be one supreme directing minister who should plan all the operations of government and direct all the departments of administration so far as to make them co-operate zealously and actively with his desires, even though contrary to their own.'

George III was, as Fox remarked, 'his own unadvised Prime Minister'. But it was paradoxical that Pitt the younger, with whom the King found himself more often in agreement than any other of his prime ministers, should have engrossed so many of the powers claimed by that monarch into his own office. In particular the general supervision of individual ministers, hitherto exercised by the Crown, passed to the Prime Minister. In 1792, Pitt secured the dismissal of the Lord Chancellor, Thurlow, who had criticized his policies in Parliament. As a result of the new Cabinet solidarity which now became the rule, the principle of collective responsibility was born. When North resigned in 1782, his entire Cabinet resigned with him. Such a convention naturally works to the advantage of the Prime Minister of the day and, except for the dismally abortive 'agreement to differ' of 1932 (which lasted only eight months), this principle has never been questioned.

The failure of William IV's dismissal of Melbourne in 1834 added to the Prime Minister's existing attributes that of irre-movability except by Parliament. It inaugurated the classic period of English Parliamentary Government, the end of which we may conveniently place in 1867, the year of the second Reform Bill. It was also, by a complete coincidence, the year of the publication of Walter Bagehot's great work, *The English Constitution*, and also incidentally of Karl Marx's *Das Kapital*. If Bagehot's views seem ironical to us, his book was nevertheless the best contemporary assessment of that exceptional thirty years.

The chief virtue which Bagehot found in the British Constitution was its flexibility, the way in which the 'efficient' parts (Cabinet and House of Commons) worked behind a screen provided by the 'dignified' parts (Monarchy and House of Lords). Bagehot believed that the real sovereignty lay with the Commons whose functions were (i) to control and criticize the executive, (ii) to provide a forum for the discussion of grievances, and (iii) virtually to nominate the prime minister. The Commons, according to Bagehot, created the Cabinet and controlled it thereafter, thus making England in effect a 'disguised republic'. This is still the theory upon which our government operates, but, as Richard Crossman has admitted in his introduction to Bagehot's work, 'this has now become part of the constitutional myth'.

Our awareness of the myth should make us cautious in accepting Bagehot's scathing remarks on the American Constitution, which incorporates *in toto* Montesquieu's theory of the separation of powers. Because it is based on a written constitution, the American system is necessarily a rigid one, difficult to reform, and only capable of working when the component parts possess the will to make it work. The British Constitution has never been based on the separation of powers, though it has from time to time attempted to evolve safeguards. The Stuart experience made politicians anxious to safeguard the independence of the judges and this was one of the objects of the Act of Settlement of 1701. But of the executive, the legislature and the judiciary, the real power in this country has always (since the civil war) lain between the executive and the legislature. At present, dominance lies with the executive as a direct result of the emergence of the Cabinet as a powerful factor; even Bagehot described the Cabinet as 'the lynchpin of the Constitution'.

Bagehot's analysis of constitutional power was rapidly overtaken by events; the power which he assigned to the Cabinet as a whole was before long assumed by the prime minister. But his ideas were really valuable in that they distinguished between 'the dignified and the efficient parts of the constitution' or, as he elsewhere put it, between the 'living reality' and the 'paper description'. The unwritten character of the British Constitution enables it to adapt more easily to changing circumstances than a written constitution on the American pattern. But it also disguises the shape and importance of the changes which do take place and creates the danger that the traditional checks and balances may be rendered antiquated and impotent. New safeguards may have to be provided from time to time.

The circumstances which so completely changed the balance of political power in the later nineteenth century was the extension of the franchise which came with dramatic suddenness. In 1867, the electorate was doubled at one stroke and in 1884 it was increased by a further 67 per cent. This resulted directly in the development of the great mass parties and of the Irish Home Rule party, whose effect on Parliamentary government was so disruptive.

The long-term effects predicted by the intellectuals varied. John Stuart Mill in his essay on 'Representative Government', written in 1861, stated that 'the proper office of a representative assembly is to watch and control the Government; to throw the light of publicity on its acts; to compel a full exposition and justification of all of them which anyone considers questionable; to censure them if found condemnable; and if the men who compose the Government abuse their trust or fulfil it in a manner which conflicts with the deliberate sense of the nation, to expel them from office and either expressly or virtually to appoint their successors'. In Mill's optimistic view the division of powers which he mistakenly thought lay at the root of the British Constitution could best be preserved by 'trusting the people'. He believed in electoral reform (rather oddly) as a bulwark against the tyranny of the majority. Bagehot proposed to avert the same tyranny by preserving the existing system. Although Richard Crossman has pointed out that 'whenever proportional representation has been tried it has fulfilled his (Bagehot's) prediction that it would undermine the independence of the MP and increase the powers of the party managers who control the electoral lists', this has tended to happen in England anyway, even without proportional representation.

Lord Holland's remark in 1830 that 'party seems to be no more' has, as R. T. McKenzie says in his book *The British Political Parties*, 'a mocking echo in our own day. Superficially at least, party is now everything.' The contrast between the party system in 1830 and today could not be sharper. Between 1830 and 1966, the electorate increased from about 220,000 to 36 million, and the MP who in 1830 represented an average of 330 voters now represents some 56,000. The result has been that it is impossible nowadays to contest an election with any hope of success without the endorsement and financial backing of a political party. In September 1830 the Treasury could analyse the 656 MPS as follows—friends . . . 311; moderate ultras . . . 37; doubtful favourable . . . 37; very doubtful . . . 24; foes . . . 188; violent ultras . . . 25; doubtful unfavourable . . . 23; the Huskisson party . . . 11. Today power lies outside Parliament and imposes on MPS a rigid discipline which rules out any such caprice. 'Your representative owes you not his industry alone but his judgement', Burke had told his constituents in his speech to the Electors of Bristol in 1774, 'and he betrays you instead of serving you if he sacrifices it to your opinion. Authoritative instructions which the member is bound blindly and implicitly to obey are utterly unknown to the laws of the land and against the tenor of our constitution.'In the nineteenth century a few (such as Lord Acton) fulminated against party from the first; most preferred to express their contempt by ignoring the phenomenon altogether. Bagehot, for instance, noted in 1867 that 'the power of leaders over their followers is strictly and wisely limited; they can take their followers but a little way and that only in certain directions'. Indeed this was true at the time that Bagehot was writing. But within twenty years of the second Reform Bill it had ceased to have any validity: Joseph Chamberlain and Randolph Churchill were proposing to give the dominant power in each party to the mass movements, and Ostrogorski was gloomily predicting the rise of 'caucus rule' on the ruins of the British Constitution. In 1876, only fifteen years after Mill's optimistic essay on 'Representative Government', only nine years after the publication of Bagehot's *English Constitution*, Anthony Trollope could write cynically in his novel *The Prime Minister* that, 'Had some inscrutable decree of fate made it certain—with a certainty not to be disturbed—that no candidate would be returned to Parliament who did not assert the earth to be triangular, there would rise immediately a clamorous assertion of triangularity among political aspirants'.

The effect of the intensification of party on political life was immediately obvious. In the mid-nineteenth century the House of Commons made and unmade governments without being dissolved. No Prime Minister could ever rely completely on the loyalty of his supporters and governments when the largest majorities on paper were liable to be put out at any time by these same supporters. Peel in 1846, Russell in 1851, Derby in 1852, Aberdeen in 1855, Palmerston in 1858, Derby in 1859 and Russell in 1866, all resigned after serious defeats in the House of Commons and were replaced by their opponents without a dissolution. Between 1832 and 1867, not a single government survived the life of a whole Parliament from one general election to another. Russell's fall in 1851 for instance was due directly to the desertion of the Peelites and the Irish Party following upon his denunciation of the Catholic hierarchy—a classic example of the importance of issues of principle in mid-nineteenth century politics. True, elections often resulted shortly after, but it is significant that 'meeting Parliament'—in the sense of asking for a vote of confidence from Parliament even after an electoral defeat—was considered to be not only politically feasible but constitutionally desirable. Disraeli's achievement in 1867 in passing the Reform Bill without a majority, by drawing the radicals away from Gladstone, showed what could be done. But in 1868 it was Disraeli himself, followed by Gladstone in 1874, who initiated the practice of accepting the defeat at the hands of the electorate without 'meeting Parliament'. The last occasion on which anything like 'meeting Parliament' could be said to have occurred was in January 1924 when Baldwin did so in the hope that the universal terror which a Labour government would inspire, even after Labour's success at the polls a month before, would keep him in power with the support of the Liberal Parliamentary Party; he was disillusioned and within days the Tories were defeated by 72 votes.

In the golden age of the mid-nineteenth century, the fluidity of party was further demonstrated by the refusal of governments to treat every issue as a vote of confidence. During the premiership of Russell and Palmerston, between 1850 and 1865, the government was defeated on average ten times in each session without resigning. Russell had to face no less than twelve 'revolts' by a majority of his supporters and in fact the whip was only imposed in about two divisions out of three. True party divisions, in which something like nine-tenths of government supporters obeyed the whip accounted for 16 per cent of the total in 1850 and only 6 per cent in 1860. During this period, the House of Commons was fulfilling its classic role of checking and balancing the power of the executive. It must however be admitted that the Government's control of business or ability to keep to any time table was extremely limited.

Between 1886 and 1905, on the other hand, governments were defeated on average only once per session, and even these rare defeats were treated very seriously; in 1895, for instance, Lord Rosebery resigned after being defeated in a snap division in the Committee of Supply on the question of the army's shortage of cordite. The new attitude left it open to any Prime Minister to use the threat of a dissolution as a weapon against his own followers and against Parliament as a whole; a threat especially powerful in view of the fact that MPs have been paid since 1912 a salary which has steadily increased from £400 to £3,250.

Here was the fulfilment of Burke's sombre prediction of the result of playing off the electors against the elected. 'The executive', Burke had written, 'will have it in their choice to resort to the one or the other as may best suit the purposes of their sinister ambition. . . . If our authority is to be upheld when we coincide in opinion with his majesty's advisers, but is to be set at nought the moment it differs from them, the House of Commons will sink into a mere appendage of the administration.' And in fact governments have only twice this century been turned out by Parliament; in 1924 and in 1940, both rather exceptional cases. The process was started whereby parliamentary affairs were insensibly to become mere shadow-boxing contests between competing elites whose real power lay elsewhere.

In Bagehot's view, this abuse of power could have been and should have been prevented by the 'dignified' parts of the Constitution, which, as he said, were 'somewhat imposing and very old and rather venerable'. However, the demise of the monarchy, already in progress in Bagehot's day, was hastened by the democratization of the party system. Perhaps the last occasion on which the monarch exercised any real discretion in the choice of a Prime Minister was in 1894, when Lord Rosebery was appointed in preference to Sir William Harcourt; even this could not have been done without the connivance of a formidable conspiracy of Liberals including Morley, Asquith and Spencer. The last election controversy involving the monarch took place in 1910 when George V almost certainly refused Asquith a dissolution unless he first introduced the Parliament Bill in the House of Lords to test the reaction of that body. The same occasion marked the end of the House of Lords as an effective legislative check upon the executive.

These developments were the inevitable results of tendencies which originated in British politics long before 1867. The catalyst which dramatically accelerated the trend was the Irish party. This party, devoted solely to the cause of Home Rule (irrespective of how, with whose support, or at what cost it was achieved), had grown up in the 1870's both as a result of the extension of the franchise and also of the Ballot Act of 1872. This Act, by introducing the secret ballot, freed the Irish voter from the intimidation of his landlord who had hitherto forced him to vote for one or other of the great English political parties. So much was appreciated by Charles Stuart Parnell who perceived, in the words of his biographer, Barry O'Brien (1899), that 'an independent Irish party was the thing wanted, and this party could be elected under the Ballot Act'. Parnell saw the weakness of the British Constitution, which was the same as that of the American one, namely that it had worked up till then simply because those involved had willed it to work. There was indeed a strong understanding that members should behave as gentlemen but, as Sir Philip Magnus has pointed out, the Irish had no ambition at that time to be considered gentlemen. Taking over from the more moderate Irish Leader Isaac Butt, Parnell transformed parliamentary obstruction into a fine art, previously unknown to English history. The culmination of the campaign came in February 1882 when the Commons was kept sitting for $41\frac{1}{2}$ hours from 4 p.m. on the Monday to 9.30 a.m. on the Wednesday. Speaker Brand had to stop the debate on his own (rather doubtful) authority, and the resolution permitting the closure was immediately introduced. Parnell found imitators on both sides of the political arena; Randolph Churchill for instance became the leading spirit along with J. E. Gorst and Arthur Balfour in the so-called 'Fourth Party' which systematically obstructed almost every important bill of the Liberal government which came to power in 1880. Already the guillotine, by which a strict timetable could be imposed on all controversial bills, had had to be introduced to deal with similar obstruction in 1881. It had to be used regularly in the 1880s and 1890s, most dramatically on the Criminal Law Amendment (Ireland) Bill of 1887, on the bill to set up the Parnell Enquiry Tribunal in 1888, on the Home Rule Bill of 1893, and on the Evicted Tenants (Ireland) Bill of 1894. Later, the Tories themselves assumed the tactics of Parnell and the guillotine had to be imposed on many of the 'welfare state' bills of the pre-war Liberal government. These procedural changes were remarkably successful in achieving the objects for which they were designed: to make only one comparison, the Home Rule Bill of 1893, to which the guillotine was actually applied, took fourteen days for its introduction and second reading, while the Coal Industry Nationalisation Bill of 1946 took only two. For this reason the guillotine has been defended and used by all governments: Balfour described it as 'martial law' when it was introduced but had little compunction about using it for the controversial Education Bill of 1902; in 1914, Ramsay MacDonald told a committee of the House that the guillotine should be abolished and more time allowed for back-bench speakers, but in 1931, when he was in power, he considered that it ought to be applied to every bill. As a result of this sharp increase in the powers of the Leader of the House of Commons, Prime Ministers were not slow to arrogate the rights and the title of that office. In this capacity, Gladstone admitted, the Prime Minister 'suggests and in a great degree fixes the course of all principal matters of business'. Such was Parnell's legacy to the House of Commons, even though in the post-1945 period the post of Leader of the House has devolved upon a Senior Member of the Cabinet.

Parnell is to be thanked also for the further intensification of party. The united body of Irishmen often held the balance of power, leaving no majority even remotely predictable and obliging the other two parties to close their ranks too. While Ireland remained the main political issue, politicians had to adjust their political allegiances in response to Ireland alone and this inevitably resulted in a narrowing of other differences between both parties. In the 1880s, Gladstone's Home Rule policy, the only one which would assure him dominance over the Commons caused men as different as the Whig patrician land-owner Hartington (Devonshire) and the radical Birmingham industrialist Joseph Chamberlain to desert the Liberals. In order to oppose Home Rule, both had to some extent to surrender their other views to the strict Tory discipline; both felt uneasy about Free Trade, though from different points of view, and both in fact resigned from Balfour's Cabinet in 1902 on this very issue. This narrowing of party was the result of the Irish controversy in the 1880s; it did not follow from the nature of the Protection dispute itself—during the Protection crisis within the Tory party in 1846, Peel's Cabinet had had views much more diverse, Peel's only real supporter being Sir James Graham. The importance of the Irish question in distinguishing the Tories from their opponents is demonstrated by the obstinacy with which *The Times* and indeed most Tories described themselves as 'Unionists' right up till the late 1930s; the official title is still, rather irrelevantly, the 'Conservative and Unionist' party.

Thus defined, parties inevitably began to appeal directly to the electorate over the head of Parliament. The idea that a party should have a direct mandate from the people was first aired by Disraeli who, for his own purposes, justified his revolt against Peel in 1846 by suggesting that Peel was not entitled to introduce any fundamental change, like the repeal of the Corn Laws, without first putting it to the electorate. 'I repeat that all power is a trust,' the hero of his novel *Vivian Grey* had said; 'that we are accountable for its exercise—that from the people and for the people, all power springs and all must exist.' Until quite recently, however, the idea made little progress. In 1868, the election was dominated by Gladstone's proposal to disestablish the Irish Church and in 1906 by the Protection controversy; in both cases the revolutionary policy being put to the electorate had originated with the Prime Minister. The two elections of 1910 were both of course dominated by the House of Lords controversy. But these were as much the exception as the rule. Gladstone did not ask for a mandate for the Irish Home Rule Bill of 1886, nor did Baldwin for a return to the gold standard in 1925 or for the Trade Disputes Act in 1927. The only occasion on which such a doctrine has been explicitly adopted by a political party was in 1893 when the

Independent Labour Party incorporated in their statutes that the Parliamentary Party should be governed directly by the annual conference. In general, Prime Ministers have fallen back on the mandate theory only when it has seemed tactically convenient for them to do so. Hence the cynicism of Disraeli's novel *Coningsby*: ' "A sound Conservative government', said Taper musingly, 'I understand: Tory men and Whig measures" '.

'The object of oratory alone', Macaulay wrote, 'is not truth but persuasion.'[1] The new party managers were not slow to realize the value of Macaulay's maxim that, given the need to appeal directly to the electorate, it was easier to project a personality than an idea. And so from the moment the electorate achieved any significant size, one man came in the mind of the nation to represent an entire government and that man had of course to be the Prime Minister. The first to explore this philosophy was Peel, in many respects the most 'modern' Prime Minister before Gladstone. He ensured that his 'Tamworth Manifesto', the subject of his election address to his constituents was widely publicized in *The Times,* the *Morning Post* and the *Morning Advertiser*. It was never spoken nor printed separately. The election of 1841 was fought in some measure at least on the contrasting personalities of Peel and Melbourne. Palmerston traded even more on his public image; the English jingoists had always liked to pick on a hero (as they had done for instance with Chatham) and Palmerston, who was in any case a flamboyant character, made full use of this, especially against Derby and Disraeli in 1857. Gladstone wrote later of this election: 'It was not an election like that of 1831 when Grey sought a judgement on reform, nor like that of 1852 when the issue was the controversy of protection. The country was to decide not on the Canton River, but on whether it would or would not have Palmerston for Prime Minister.'

As personality contests, the election campaigns between Gladstone and Disraeli have no equal in the nineteenth century.

[1] T. B. Macaulay: *Essay on Athenian Orators.*

The Midlothian Campaign of 1879-80 caused a sensation in the national press and offended Queen Victoria, who later rebuked Gladstone for indulging in 'popular agitation by addressing public meetings from time to time at places with which (he) was not connected'. This superbly stage-managed campaign in a single constituency cost Lord Rosebery £50,000 compared with a total of £33,000 spent by the Liberal Party Central Fund on the whole of the rest of the country, and although its effect on this mainly rural seat was small, the press coverage which it received undoubtedly increased the indignation of the industrial masses with Disraeli's government and made Gladstone's victory more complete than it would otherwise have been. Disraeli was prevented by the convention that peers did not make election speeches from replying, though as a good House of Commons man he would probably have thought it wrong to stump the country at election times. His two greatest non-parliamentary efforts at mass oratory at Manchester and the Crystal Palace were not delivered at election times. Midlothian endowed Gladstone with huge political authority in his own right. Even though Hartington was officially Leader of the Liberal Party (Gladstone having resigned in 1875 to indulge in theological pursuits), the Queen was unable to avoid having Gladstone as Prime Minister (Gladstone replying when asked what office he would accept under Hartington that he would rest content with Number Ten). Bagehot tells the story of a bad speaker in the election of 1868 who, when asked how he got on as a candidate, answered, 'Oh, when I do not know what to say, I say "Gladstone" and they are sure to cheer and I have time to think'. Among the factors which caused the emergence of the modern Prime Minister in the later nineteenth century we must number the conflict between Disraeli and Gladstone, which fixed the attention of the country on the party leader rather than on the party, thus making the leader indispensable to the party. Could Gladstone have retained the loyalty of his party in the 1880s without the personal power which he thus possessed?

Prime Ministers of this century have tended to follow the Gladstone tradition. Lloyd George fought the 'khaki' election of 1918 purely on his personal record. His views mattered little and still less did those of his colleagues. Lord Beaverbrook has appositely remarked that Lloyd George did not care which way the vehicle was travelling so long as he was in the driving seat; but he was enabled to do this only by the immense personal reputation which he had built up. In 1945 the Tories made a mistake in trying to do the same thing by fighting an election almost entirely on Churchill's personal record. It backfired, because people were sceptical of Churchill's abilities as a peace-time politician.

By 1922 the Chanak crisis, in which Britain was nearly involved in a war with Turkey, in fact convinced the public that this was true of Lloyd George as well.

Ramsay MacDonald was an even more remarkable case. The only colourful personality in his government, he quickly established his reputation. In 1931 he appealed on radio for a 'doctor's mandate' and secured (for the first time in forty years of controversy) a mandate for Protection and devaluation—and incidentally the largest parliamentary majority since political parties began. The result was that he built up sufficient prestige outside Parliament, the Cabinet, and the party to make himself indispensable to the National Government, even though he had lost his party and his mental powers had begun to wane. This was a unique achievement—previously those Prime Ministers who had lost their party (Peel in 1846 and Lloyd George in 1922) had found themselves in the position of generals without armies, powerless in the field. Even Stanley Baldwin concealed behind the useful façade of being a man 'of the utmost insignificance' (Curzon's alleged words) great shrewdness and political skill; Lloyd George, who found few equals in his time, called him 'the most formidable political antagonist whom I have ever encountered'. Unenterprising Baldwin certainly was, but his attitude was electorally the most rewarding that he could have adopted. 'My worst enemy', he told his official biographer, 'could never say that I did not understand the people of England.'

In the last eighty years, British politics have seen two important developments in party politics, the tendency of parties to appeal over the head of Parliament to the electorate and the parallel tendency for party leaders to embody their parties in the eyes of that electorate.

The theory, as always, was slow to catch up on the practice. As 'A Conservative' wrote in *The Times* of April 2, 1964, 'Humbug is part of politics, a convention of "the British way of life", something which the public expect the politicians to give them as their due. It often performs a valuable function for a party, a class, or the nation at large by enabling them not to see, or to pretend not to see, unwelcome changes in the real world until sentiment and habits have become sufficiently adapted to them. In this way it acts like the fluid which the snail exudes to mend its broken shell. But though healthy and preservative when applied at the right time and for the right purposes, humbug can become deleterious and even fatal if it is not shed when the time is past and those purposes fulfilled.'

The office of the Prime Minister was not mentioned in statute before the Chequers Estate Act of 1917, nor was the Cabinet mentioned before the Ministers of the Crown Act of 1937. More important, politics were, until recently, dominated by what Professor Birch has called the Liberal ideal of the Constitution. This ideal was that the government was responsible to the electorate only through the House of Commons. This had been true in Gladstone's time: Gladstone himself was an instrument in altering it. By the time his pupil and biographer John Morley, who was a member of every Liberal Cabinet from 1886 to 1914, was writing, it certainly was untrue. 'The Cabinet', John Morley still believed 'is answerable immediately to the majority of the House of Commons and ultimately to the electors whose will creates that majority. The only real responsibility is to the House of Commons.' The 8th Duke of Devonshire, who sat in both

Tory and Liberal Cabinets, put the ideal even more directly: addressing the Lords in September 1893, he said: 'Parliament makes or unmakes our ministries, it revises their actions. Ministries may make peace and war but they do so at pain of instant dismissal by Parliament from office, and in affairs of internal administration the power of Parliament is equally direct. It can dismiss a ministry if it is too extravagant or too economical; it can dismiss a ministry because its government is too stringent or too lax. It does actually and practically in every way govern England, Scotland and Ireland.' This was still the assumption on which Parliament has operated, and it could hardly by then have been more inaccurate. In 1934, even, a committee of the House of Commons on Government considered as basic to British government the idea that 'the only form of self-government worthy of the name is government through ministers responsible to an elected legislature'.

It was not not till the 1930s that people as a whole began to recognize the anomalous state of the English Constitution. Lord Chief Justice Hewart wrote *The New Despotism* in 1929, in which he criticized the 'increasing incapacity of the House of Commons to perform its work'. Ramsay Muir and the Webbs followed suit. W. I. Jennings wrote in 1934 that 'the backbench member is almost impotent in the House'. But at the end of the nineteenth century it was only a perceptive few who saw the significance of the changes that were then taking place. Sir Henry Maine in his *Popular Government*, Ostrogorski's *Democracy and the Organisation of Political Parties,* and Goldwyn Smith's *A Trip to England,* all predicted as a result of the extensions of the franchise, first a cynical auction of policies between parties bidding for popular favour, and secondly the end of the independence of the individual MP. By the 1930s, both of these predictions were uncomfortably near to fulfilment.

'How important singleness and unity are in political action, no one, I imagine, can doubt. . . . The interlaced character of human affairs requires a single determining energy. . . . The excellence of the British constitution is that it has achieved this unity, that in it the sovereign power is single, possible, and good.' Bagehot's words, like Lord Holland's, have a mocking echo when quoted by Ostrogorski who summed up his historical analysis of party up till the 1890s as follows: 'Formerly the leader of the party was only *primus inter pares*; now he is a general in command of an army. . . . Raised above the level crowd of MPs, the leaders now lean directly on the great mass of voters, whose feelings of loyalty go straight to the leaders over the heads of the Members. . . . This being so, the elections have assumed the character of personal plebiscites, each constituency voting not so much for this or that candidate as for Mr Gladstone or against Lord Beaconsfield or Lord Salisbury.'

CHAPTER III

THE RESOURCES OF THE PRIME MINISTER

'The head of the British Government', Gladstone said, 'is not a Grand Vizier. He has no powers, properly so called over his colleagues: on the rare occasions when a Cabinet determines its course by the votes of its members, his vote counts only as one of theirs. But they are appointed and dismissed by the sovereign on his advice. In a perfectly organized administration such, for example, as that of Sir Robert Peel in 1841-6, nothing of great importance is matured or would even be projected in any department without his personal cognizance and any weighty business would commonly go to him before being submitted to the Cabinet.' Even as early as Gladstone's day the Prime Minister had become something more than *primus inter pares*. However the theory that Parliament controls not only the Cabinet but the Prime Minister as well has been preserved to this day, like the many myths of party politics, as part of the 'British way of life'. In 1918, for example, the Machinery of Government Committee found that the functions of the Cabinet were (i) the final determination of the policy to be submitted to Parliament, (ii) the supreme control of the national executive in accordance with the policy prescribed by Parliament, and (iii) the continuous co-ordination and delimitation of the activities of the several departments of state. Yet even at the time that this was written, most members of the committee must have been aware that this was simply not happening.

The tendency for Prime Ministers to dominate their Cabinets has been greatly accelerated in this century by changes in the structure of the Cabinet and the creation of the Cabinet office. These gave a permanent and institutional basis to powers which some Prime Ministers had exercised before by virtue of their own personalities. There had always been strong Prime Ministers and weak ones. 'There is not and cannot be any authoritative definition of the precise relation of the Prime Minister to his colleagues', Asquith wrote.[1] 'The office of the Prime Minister is what its holder chooses and is able to make of it.' This meant that the power of the Prime Minister could only progress by a dotted line. The effect of the structural changes was to make it into a broad straight line.

Peel, whose administration we have seen Gladstone describe as a 'perfectly organised one', was the first to exercise a detailed supervision over ministries as well as ministers. In 1842 he, and not the Chancellor of the Exchequer, introduced the Budget. In 1846 he carried through the repeal of the Corn Laws against the whole of the rest of the Cabinet except Graham. But Peel's power rested on his own personal qualities, and his immediate successors, lacking those qualities, did not provide the same degree of leadership. In 1859-60, when the Queen found herself in disagreement with the Prime Minister Palmerston over foreign policy, she referred the decisions of the Prime Minister and the Foreign Secretary to the Cabinet as a whole. Gladstone's Budget of 1860 was not referred to Palmerston, who found parts of it repugnant. 'Nobody thought of consulting Palmerston first, but brought his measure at once to Cabinet', Gladstone later remarked. The ascendancy of Gladstone and Disraeli in the great age of personality politics established the principle that the Prime Minister was by then a great deal more than *primus inter pares*. Disraeli, who realized fully the strength of his own position, would generally announce his own view at the beginning of each Cabinet meeting and then hold to it against all comers. He believed

[1] *Fifty years of Parliament*, London: Cassell, 1926

in a strong initiative by the Prime Minister, criticizing Liverpool, for instance, in his novel *Coningsby* as 'the Arch-Mediocrity, who presided rather than ruled over this Cabinet of Mediocrities'. Gladstone on the other hand did not bulldoze his Cabinet, not at any rate until his last years, but he got his own way nevertheless. He had, as Stansfield said, 'a wonderful combination of imperiousness . . . and of deference'.

Balfour was not as good at managing people as either Gladstone or Disraeli, but he made up for this by a reserve of political ruthlessness which he drew on in 1903 when he brought about the resignation of five members of his Cabinet, including two of the most powerful, Chamberlain and Devonshire—a feat unequalled until Macmillan massacred a third of his Cabinet in 1962. Asquith on the other hand had neither ruthlessness nor persuasiveness in abundance. Nevertheless he was far from being a nonentity and Balfour gave him a just tribute in calling him 'an arbitrator, an eminently fair-minded judge, a splendid chairman of committee'.

It is surprising to hear from many who served under him, including Beaverbrook, that Lloyd George was tolerant in Cabinet. Beaverbrook wrote that 'his team play was perfect the moment he was made a captain'.[1] As a body the power of the War Cabinet at this time was absolute, chiefly because of its small size. 'What is a government for, except to dictate? If it does not dictate, then it is not a government', Lloyd George retorted when a Labour MP described a Cabinet of five as a disguised dictatorship.

But the real question is the degree to which the decisions of the Cabinet were in fact those of Lloyd George. It is not cynical to suggest that Lloyd George preserved harmony in his Cabinet by dealing with some of the more controversial issues outside Cabinet. The important fact to realize about Prime Ministers before Lloyd George is that although some of them may have been dominating characters who acted very arbitrarily at times,

[1] *Politicians and the War.*

they left no mantle for their weaker successors to assume. Lloyd George's contribution to the office of the Prime Minister was to place the powers which he exercised by virtue of his personality on an institutional basis by setting up the Cabinet office. The result was that thereafter even an apparently unassuming Prime Minister like Attlee possessed immense powers derived not from his own personality but by virtue of the office which he held and the staff which serviced it.

The actual reason for the formation of the Cabinet Office was the pressure of work during the First World War. Asquith tried to maintain his detached, conciliating role even in wartime. He failed and it quickly became apparent to all but Asquith that, at a time when rapid and unequivocal decisions were required, there had to be some means of registering and implementing those decisions which had actually been made. As it happened the embryo of Lloyd George's Cabinet organization was already there in the form of the Committee of Imperial Defence, a committee of the Prime Minister and other ministers of his own choice, with chiefs of staff in attendance; this committee had its own secretariat. Despite the existence of the Committee of Imperial Defence which had been set up by the Conservative Government in 1904, and despite Kitchener's membership of the Cabinet, liaison between the civil and military powers was notoriously bad during the first two years of the war. Kitchener quarrelled endlessly with the 'twenty-three gentlemen with whom I am hardly acquainted' (as he called them), and Fisher resigned as First Sea Lord after a quarrel with Churchill. The inefficiency of the old order put Lloyd George in power, and he immediately appointed Col. Hankey to form a Cabinet Secretariat.

Whether or not it was intended to be permanent, the Cabinet Office soon became indispensable. It first appeared in the estimates in 1917; after the war it did not disappear. The Machinery of Government Committee of 1918 recommended that it should be retained 'for the purpose of collecting and putting into shape the agenda, of providing the information and material necessary for its deliberations and of drawing up the results for communication to the departments concerned'. Most significant of all, Bonar Law, who had rashly promised in the election campaign of 1922 to abolish the Cabinet Office, found himself unable to do more than cut its personnel from 144 to 38.

The tendency towards Prime Ministerial government which the Cabinet Office represented was illustrated by the parallel development of Lloyd George's own personal Secretariat to supply his unquenchable thirst for information. 'Of secretaries', said Thomas Jones, the deputy head of the Cabinet Office, 'Lloyd George could never have enough.' Unlike the Cabinet Office, which lived in Whitehall Gardens, the personal Secretariat was housed in the basement of 10 Downing Street and in a Nissen Hut which Lloyd George had built in the Garden of 10 Downing Street: hence the sobriquet 'the Garden Suburb'. Its staff were not necessarily recruited through the civil service. In due course it was abolished and the Prime Minister was personally served by a small number of civil service private secretaries. As far as effective power is concerned the distinction between the Cabinet Office and the Number Ten staff has always been somewhat blurred. Although the theory goes that the Cabinet Secretariat is somehow responsible to the Cabinet as a body, it is difficult to see how in practice it can take its orders from an assembly of over twenty people. In fact it takes orders from the chairman of the Cabinet, the Prime Minister. In an interview with Norman Hunt on BBC radio on February 24, 1964, Harold Wilson admitted in fact that this was so: 'The Cabinet Secretariat', he said, 'has never been responsible to or under the control of the Cabinet . . .; the Cabinet Secretariat would provide advice for the Prime Minister on what might be going wrong and on policy.' The Prime Minister personally appoints the Secretary to the Cabinet, and there is no doubt that it is to the Prime Minister that he is in fact responsible. Lloyd George's 'Garden Suburb', was pulled down by Bonar Law, but it reappeared in practice, if not in strict fact, several times in the course of the next thirty years. The Cabinet Office remained all the while. Mr Wilson, in the course of the 1964 election campaign, said on several occasions that he would restore the name as well as the fact of the Prime Minister's Secretariat. In the face of a storm of pious indignation he did not in fact do so, but it was nevertheless his professed aim to strengthen Number Ten in this way. 'I more than once said', he told an interviewer on a television documentary in January 1965, 'that I thought Number Ten should be a power house and not a monastery. It's important that a Prime Minister must know all that's going on. I've certainly no complaints on that score.'

Ironically enough, Hankey, though he saw the constitutional implications of the Prime Minister's Secretariat, seemed to have little idea of the scope of the Cabinet Office and even to have thought that it might limit the Prime Minister's power. In *The Supreme Command*,[1] he wrote that 'If anything the Secretariat would seem to act as a check on independent action as it is its duty to communicate the decisions to the Prime Minister who is called upon to act. When the decision is written, it must be written clearly. It must be difficult for the Prime Minister to overstep it.' The practice was very different. In the past, the power of any Prime Minister had always been limited by his own capacity to control. 'A Prime Minister who is the senior partner in every department as well as president of the whole is almost, if not quite, an impossibility', Rosebery considered. 'Men of ordinary physique and discretion cannot be President and live, if the strain be not somehow relieved', said the American President Wilson; 'we shall be obliged always to be picking our chief magistrates from among wise and prudent athletes—a small class.' In mundane terms, the Prime Ministers of this century have on the whole been older and weaker than their aristocratic predecessors of the eighteenth and nineteenth centuries. MacDonald, Baldwin, Churchill and Eden and Macmillan were all seriously ill while in office. The Cabinet Office enables any

[1] London: George Allen & Unwin, 1961.

Prime Minister to perform a task which is formidable, even for a healthy man.

Provided that he can undertake the work involved, the large size of modern Cabinets makes it easier for the Prime Minister to dominate. Of course, the trend to larger Cabinets was not deliberately engineered with this end in mind; it was the result of the increase in the number of departments. With the widening of the scope of government, new ministries were created and it became difficult on political grounds to exclude from the Cabinet a man whose predecessor had sat there; this has in this century for the most part only been possible in wartime. Disraeli in 1874 had a Cabinet of twelve to fourteen, thirteen at its inception, admittedly small even by the standards of the day; but later Cabinets were by consensus of opinion too large. Asquith's coalition Cabinet was twenty-two in 1915 and had grown to twenty-four by 1916, and this in wartime. Attlee in more recent times had a Cabinet of seventeen and had originally hoped to manage with a smaller one. Before taking office in 1964, Mr Wilson had suggested that something more than fifteen and less than twenty-three would be appropriate, but the realities of power convinced him that twenty-three (now reduced to twenty-one) was even more appropriate, which was, Enoch Powell thought, 'a bit on the high side'.

No Cabinet of this size can easily come to a decision. Disputes are inevitable. Asquith had to spend much of his time settling quarrels between ministers, many of them involving McKenna, who found it difficult not to interfere with other departments. For example, in 1909 McKenna wanted many more battleships than the strong 'economy' block in the Cabinet (Churchill, Lloyd George, and others) would allow. In 1911 he quarrelled with Haldane not only over the role of the army in Britain's defence policy, but also over its internal organization. During the first war Asquith had to arbitrate in such disputes as the shell-design controversy between the War Office and the Ministry of Munitions, Churchill's row with Fisher, and Lloyd George's with

Robertson. By tradition no vote is taken at Cabinet meetings. Many members of the Cabinet will be reluctant to take issue with the Prime Minister, who can therefore determine the agenda within very broad limits indeed. In practice much of the effective work must therefore be done in committees of the Cabinet.

In the Labour Government of 1945–50, the huge legislative programme made it necessary to delegate a great deal of work to such committees. A number of permanent committees were founded, including the general purposes committee, committees on defence, economic policy, social legislation, foreign policy, etc., and also the extremely important legislation committee which dealt with the actual business of getting this programme through Parliament. Many 'ad hoc' committees have also been formed to deal with specific issues as they arose, Indian Independence, Suez, the Common Market, and Rhodesia, to name only a few. Many of these, and certainly the more important ones are chaired by the Prime Minister and all report to him as chairman of the Cabinet. The result is that the Prime Minister is the only member of the Cabinet who is informed of everything. He can take on the role of co-ordinator because the Cabinet Office places at his disposal information on every single Cabinet activity, while ordinary members have detailed knowledge only of those matters dealt with in the various committees of which they were members or of their own departments. Lord Kilmuir, in his memoirs,[1] gave general praise to Macmillan's chairmanship of the Cabinet but commented that 'now and again the Cabinet was consulted at too late a stage in the evolution of some important line of policy; he seemed to forget that many of us had not been present at the Cabinet committee concerned with the topic'.

Problems of defence had brought the new Cabinet Office into existence and it was therefore in the realm of defence that their effect was most rapidly felt. Clemenceau's dictum that war is much too serious an affair to be left to the military was seen everywhere at work under Lloyd George. Even before Lloyd

---

[1] *Political Adventure.*

George, the Committee of Imperial Defence, on which both ministers and professional warriors sat, had acted as a personal advisory body to the Prime Minister. It had a permanent secretariat and its proceedings were minuted some twelve years before those of the Cabinet itself. During the Agadir crisis of 1911, the important decisions were made in the CID and not referred to the Cabinet at all, and the Cabinet protested very strongly when it found out two months later. But this was still far from the direct subordination of chiefs of staff to the Prime Minister or even to their political departmental heads, as became apparent when the First World War brought a rash of quarrels between civil and military. The result of these quarrels was the withdrawal of effective power from both civil and military into the hands of the Prime Minister. Because none of the heads of the defence departments were included in Lloyd George's small War Cabinet of between five and seven ministers, the Prime Minister was able to deal much more directly with each chief of staff in turn. In his memoirs of the 1914–1918 war, the Chief of Imperial General Staff, Sir William Robertson, wrote that, 'The constant aim of the new Prime Minister was to take the military direction of the war more and more into his own hands, and to have carried out military plans of his own devising, which, more often than not, were utterly at variance with the views of his responsible advisers'.

Lloyd George by-passed the generals, by appointing his own personal military advisers. It was for just this reason that Smuts was invited to join the War Cabinet. Robertson was consistently undermined and eventually replaced by the more compliant Wilson with reduced powers. Lloyd George was no less in command of the Navy. When the Admiralty resisted the Cabinet's demands for the introduction of convoys to protect merchant shipping against the total submarine warfare which the Germans had just declared, Lloyd George obtained intelligence directly from junior officers. Armed with this he 'descended', in the words of Beaverbrook, 'upon the Admiralty and seated himself in the First Lord's chair'. Convoys were forthwith introduced, and by the end of the year both the First Lord and the First Sea Lord had resigned, the latter to be replaced by a number of nonentities who were never more than administrators.

The full potential of the Cabinet Office in enabling a Prime Minister to run Britain's defence was only realized during the Second War. As Prime Minister with the additional title of Minister of Defence, Churchill had more power than any other Prime Minister in this century, including Lloyd George. As Minister of Defence he inaugurated a department with only a handful of secretaries and no powers at all, but was immediately able to assume full powers by using the Military Secretariat of the Cabinet. Asquith had believed that it was not the job of the Prime Minister to 'play the part of the amateur strategist or foist his opinions on men who had made soldiering the study of their life'. No such inhibitions troubled either Lloyd George or Churchill, both of whom interested themselves in the minutest details of the running of the war. Both for instance, with varying degrees of success, championed the cause of a second front, Lloyd George in Salonika and Churchill in Italy. No one doubted that Churchill had assumed full military direction of the war.

In *The Second World War*, Churchill himself described the extent of his powers: 'The key change which occurred on taking over was of course the supervision and direction of the Chief of Staffs Committee by a minister with undefined powers. As this minister was also the Prime Minister, he had all the rights inherent in that office, including very wide powers of selection and removal of all professional and political personages.' Thus he dealt personally with allied generals, especially Eisenhower, though here he did not always get his way. In 1942 there was strong criticism in Parliament of the close link between Churchill and his chiefs of staff; Churchill asked for a vote of confidence and the mutterings ended. Like Lloyd George, Churchill also gathered around him a number of personal advisers. In addition to the Secretary to the War Cabinet, he had a personal staff officer (Ismay), a scientific officer (Cherwell), and many others. In Churchill's hands, subordination of home policy to the task of winning the war meant the use of the Cabinet as the machine which made the economic and political arrangements at home for the military policy which Churchill adopted abroad.

After the war Attlee also took the title of Minister of Defence (for a year), as did Churchill when he once more became Prime Minister in 1951. It was symbolic of the degree to which the Prime Minister had come to dictate defence policy. In wartime a strong line has to be taken by the Prime Minister; but the Cabinet Office has ensured that such powers can be exercised by a peacetime Prime Minister as well. The Defence White Paper of 1946 recommended that the Prime Minister retain his supreme responsibility for defence and remain chairman of the Defence Committee of the Cabinet. Attlee, although not as dominant a personality as Churchill, meant to use these powers to the full; in 1946 it was he who ordered the production of the Atom Bomb. Although Attlee soon shed the Ministry of Defence to A. V. Alexander, the small staff which an independent Ministry of Defence was allotted provided an important limit to the Minister's power. The military failures during the Suez crisis showed, however, that in practice Prime Ministers had not maintained the same close relations with their chiefs of staff as Churchill had with his during the war. The result was a new White Paper in 1958, which stressed the principle that the Prime Minister was a permanent and ex-officio member of the Defence Committee of the Cabinet as well as being its chairman, but it still failed to lay down any precise formula for the relations between civil and military. Nevertheless it did prove to be the start of greater things.

By 1964, the reorganization of the Defence departments into a unified ministry under a single Secretary of State was completed. This system has yet to stand the test of war, but the lesson of the last fifty years is that in the absence of any formal arrangement the effective power lies with him who has the best administrative resources to exercise it—the Prime Minister and his Secretariat.

The Prime Minister presides over all defence and foreign policy committees of the Cabinet. Sometimes the Cabinet has been kept in ignorance. Between 1912 and 1914 for instance, only Asquith and Grey knew of the Anglo-French military 'conversations' which in effect committed Britain to support France in any major war with Germany. But until the last moment the Cabinet never knew that its freedom of choice had been limited in this way. Cabinet Committees do not always have all the information that they require on defence or foreign policy. Backbenchers hardly ever do. Neither of these subjects is sufficiently often debated in the House of Commons. The infrequency of debates, together with the difficulty of adequately discussing the basic issues in the medium of a Parliamentary debate, make it impossible for the legislature to exercise a real control of the executive. Nor can such issues be tackled at Question Time— even though opponents of the government's attitude to the Vietnam war have found this a convenient method of airing their grievances. The truth is that any proper review by the House of Commons of the vital fields of defence and foreign policy can only be handled by specialist committees of the House of Commons devoted to those subjects and these are not envisaged by the present government.

Important issues of foreign policy are often difficult to separate from those of defence, and the same trend can be observed in this sphere. Increasingly the Prime Minister has come to dominate foreign policy too. Strong Prime Ministers have always had a controlling interest in the foreign field, though again they left no official mantle for their successors to assume. No one doubted that Disraeli ran England's foreign policy between 1874 and 1880. Disraeli treated Derby, the Foreign Secretary, throughout as a subordinate. In 1875 he gave his Cabinet little time to discuss the purchase of the Suez Canal and carried it through in opposition not only to Derby but to Cairns, Northcote and most of the rest of the Cabinet as well. During the exceedingly complicated negotiations which led up to the Treaty of Berlin, Derby followed a pro-Russian line even to the extent of feeding Count Shuvalov, the Russian Ambassador, with details of the deliberations of the Cabinet. At the Congress of Berlin, Disraeli himself was the chief representative of Britain and in signing the final treaty as 'Prime Minister of Britain' he was responsible for one of the few official references to the office which he held. Disraeli achieved much personal popularity at first by his handling of foreign policy, but when Parliament and the electorate turned on him for the disasters in Afghanistan and South Africa, they were recognizing that a change had taken place in the traditional concept of responsibility. Salisbury, who was Foreign Secretary from 1878 to 1880, insisted on doubling the offices of Prime Minister and Foreign Secretary in his first administration (1885-6) and in his third (1895-1902) until 1900. After Salisbury, MacDonald was the only Prime Minister to be Foreign Secretary as well. But this had ceased to be necessary, as Prime Ministers have found that it is as easy to run the foreign policy of Britain from Downing Street as it is from Whitehall. Perhaps the only Foreign Secretary since Grey who ran his own department as much in practice as all Foreign Secretaries do in theory was Ernest Bevin. And as one official told Bevin when he took over, 'We have not been the Foreign Office for years. We have been merely a post office for Number Ten Downing Street.'

This state of affairs originated, like the defence reorganizations, in Lloyd George's time. Again it was Lloyd George who provided an administrative basis for the powers which he actually exercised by virtue of his forceful personality. At the Peace Conference after the 1914–1918 War it was Lloyd George, Wilson and Clemenceau who made the decisions, and in this period the Prime Minister was able to dominate the Foreign Office with no difficulty. Balfour got on in any case with Lloyd George and did not argue for all his rights. Curzon got on very badly with the Prime Minister but he enjoyed the prestige of the Foreign Office; it had long been his ambition to become Foreign Secretary and he was prepared to suffer insult and injury rather than resign. Insult and injury were forthcoming in plenty from Lloyd George. Indeed, when the Prime Minister was abroad, Curzon became a mere registrar for the numerous decrees which issued from wherever Lloyd George happened to be at the time. During the Second World War, when Lloyd George was condemning the autocratic manner in which Churchill treated his ministers, he said, 'I never treated the members of my War Cabinet like this,' and then added as an afterthought, 'Oh yes, there was one—Curzon'. In 1921, for example, he by-passed the Foreign Office in order to negotiate the Treaty of Sèvres while he was staying at San Remo. The treaty contained at least two clauses objectionable to Curzon, who complained that, 'There has grown up a system in which there are in reality two foreign offices: the one for which I am responsible, and the other at No. 10'. At this point, Lord Ronaldshay in his *Life of Lord Curzon* comments, 'In the large private secretariat which he (Lloyd George) built for himself in Downing Street, he found a convenient and ever-ready agency for carrying into effect any orders which he felt moved to give'. Indeed, at the last, it was Lloyd George's autocratic behaviour which brought about his fall. During the Chanak crisis of 1922, he issued on his own authority a statement to the press which was almost a declaration of war with Turkey: the result of which was that against the advice of their leaders a majority of the Conservatives in the House of Commons withdrew their support and the coalition government fell.

Neville Chamberlain made it clear to his colleagues, as soon as he took office, that he intended to be his own Foreign Secretary. Like Lloyd George, he disliked and suspected diplomats. He steadily undermined Eden and drew all the important business to the Cabinet committee on overseas policy, of which the Prime Minister was chairman. Vansittart, who had a fanatical hatred of the dictators and whom Chamberlain feared might unduly influence Eden, was 'promoted' from his post as Permanent

Under Secretary in the Foreign Office to another as Chief Diplomatic Adviser to the Government, in which he had no powers or influence. Chamberlain supplemented the advice of professional diplomats by that of a group of personal advisers, the chief of whom was Sir Horace Wilson, who accompanied the Prime Minister on most of his diplomatic trips. Thus Chamberlain corresponded with Mussolini without Eden's knowledge; a revealing entry in his diary concerning this correspondence reads, 'I did not show my letter to the Foreign Secretary, for I had the feeling that he would object to it'. At Munich he was accompanied not by the Foreign Secretary but by his personal advisers, including Sir Horace Wilson. Throughout the crisis the Prime Minister worked through an inner Cabinet of Simon, Hoare and Halifax. The Cabinet as a whole was consulted only at very short notice and Chamberlain in fact told Parliament in his own defence that in a time of crisis a Prime Minister was entitled to ignore the opinions of his colleagues. The verdict of his own party was seen when thirty MPs who normally supported the Government, including Churchill, Eden, Cranborne, Amery and Duff Cooper, abstained. 'The Prime Minister had strong views on foreign policy, and I respect him for it', Eden had told the House of Commons after his resignation a few months earlier than Munich; 'I have strong views too'. Eden was replaced by Halifax who, as well as being more compliant, also sat in the House of Lords, leaving responsibility for expounding foreign policy in the Commons to Chamberlain.

Churchill managed his Foreign Secretaries more skilfully, first Halifax and then Eden, but there is nevertheless no doubt that real control was his. When discussing his relations with the Cabinet in *The Hinge of Fate*, Churchill remarked 'I did not suffer from any desire to be relieved of my responsibilities. All I wanted was compliance with my wishes after reasonable discussion.' What more could one desire? Churchill himself, like Disraeli, Lloyd George, and Chamberlain before him, acted as an ambassador extraordinary. Eden, who had already shown himself to be a man of strong principles, did not accompany him to Casablanca or to Moscow, nor was he present on most of Churchill's visits to Washington. On June 22, 1941, Churchill announced the policy of giving all possible aid to Russia without consulting the Cabinet, and adds (in *The Grand Alliance*) 'nor was it necessary'.

During the Suez crisis, Eden proved to be little less autocratic than Chamberlain. Eden formulated the policies followed in the Middle East. The Cabinet was consulted only hours before the ultimatum was sent and all the work was done in a Cabinet committee and within the small circle which surrounded Eden (Butler, Macmillan, Salisbury, Selwyn Lloyd and Head). Similarly the Common Market negotiations were handled by Macmillan in concert with a small group which included Butler, Home and Heath; in practice Macmillan made the decisions and Heath executed them.

The Prime Minister's personal influence is also paramount in economic policy. It is, moreover, a relatively new field of government activity and there is in consequence no tradition of resistance to the Prime Minister, as the generals resisted Lloyd George or as Eden resisted Chamberlain. During the 1914–1918 war it was necessary to control resources, but this was always strictly a means to an end; Lloyd George considered it to be of secondary and merely administrative importance and he left it to a number of ministries specially created for that purpose. Although after the 1914–1918 war an Economic Policy Committee of the Cabinet was set up, with Lloyd George in the chair, it was not until the first Labour government that the organization of the economy and the redistribution of resources was pursued, even nominally, as an end in itself. In fact Labour's policy at that time was never more than nominal. The experiment of a Committee of Civil Research, modelled on the pre-war Committee of Imperial Defence, together with its successor of 1930, the Economic Advisory Council, was a failure. But it showed the direction in which events were moving, for it worked under the personal direction of the Prime Minister who was also its chairman. On the whole the governments of the 1930s preferred to alleviate distress by means of the 'dole' than to avoid it by means of Keynesian policies, although the establishment of a Commissioner for the Special Areas and the big housing drive of the 1930s were genuine Keynesian injections of spending power. Until the second war the course of economic policy was determined rather by departmental ministers and civil servants than by any conscious direction on the part of the Prime Minister.

In 1940 a step was taken in economic policy parallel to the formation of the Cabinet Office in defence and foreign policy, with the establishment of the Central Economic Information Service, later split up into an economic and a statistical section. The services of this office were in theory equally available to any other minister as to the Prime Minister, but as it became part of the Cabinet Office, the same considerations apply here as in the diplomatic field. Churchill, in addition to this office, had his own Statistical Office headed by Lord Cherwell, in which some of the ablest advisers served: Harrod, MacDougall, Shackle, and others. This was emphatically the personal property of the Prime Minister and not part of the Civil Service. It recruited its staff independently of the Civil Service, which resented deeply the presence of 'S Branch' as it was called. Secure in Churchill's confidence, Cherwell wielded (as C. P. Snow has said) 'more direct power than any scientist in history'.

Under Attlee, the Central Statistical Office continued, as it still does, to issue a monthly digest and an annual abstract of statistics. The famous White Paper on Employment of 1944 had pronounced it to be the duty of the government to maintain a 'high and stable level of employment'. After the Fuel Crisis of 1946-7, Attlee personally took charge of economic policy. In 1947 Attlee's personal position was weakened by the disillusionment among many Labour MPs and ministers, and Cripps was given charge of a new Ministry of Economic Affairs with responsibility for planning. But although Cripps was a man of iron will he was given no department, only a small personal staff. He remained in this post for a few weeks only before succeeding Dalton as Chancellor of the Exchequer. The real power remained with the Economic Policy Committee of the Cabinet of which Attlee, primed by his Civil Service, was chairman.

Since October 1964, although not formally introducing a personal secretariat, Wilson has in fact increased the number of his personal staff. He has a number of personal economic advisers who, like Cherwell under Churchill, are not civil servants. As soon as he came to power he took on Balogh (now partly released) and Kaldor as his economic advisers. Both are dons. When he discussed this on a television documentary in January 1965, Wilson explained that he had brought into his personal staff a number of outsiders, 'one or two on the economic side, because I always felt that we should need most strengthening in the new economic departments and also of course in the fields of science and technology. So both of these sides have been strengthened and there is a very efficient machine.' The Secretary of State for Economic Affairs had found himself sandwiched between the Chancellor and the Prime Minister. Significantly enough, on July 20, 1966, it was the Prime Minister who announced the new and stringent economic restrictions to the House of Commons. This superseded the five-year plan which had been the main concern of the Department of Economic Affairs. Mr Brown, in theory the minister responsible, was not even present at the time, a fact which aroused much comment, especially in view of his reported resignation (which was rejected) soon afterwards. Three weeks after Wilson's statement Brown was transferred to the Foreign Office.[1]

The political advantages are clearly all on the Prime Minister's side. Matters of political tactics rest with him as head of the Government and leader of a big political party, and this gives him an important power over the political future of Cabinet

[1] In August 1967 Wilson assumed personal responsibility for the conduct of Economic Policy.

Ministers. The timing of the election of 1923, for example, was Baldwin's, as was the decision to fight it on the issue of protection; the Cabinet was neither pleased nor consulted, but to protest would have been to present a divided front to the electorate, damaging the party's chances in the election (which incidentally it lost). Similarly the Cabinet of the second Labour Government was cursorily told of its resignation by MacDonald, and of the formation in its stead of a National Cabinet composed of members who within a year were to 'agree to differ'.

The informal origin of the Cabinet has made it possible, in the course of two centuries, for change to occur unobserved and therefore unresisted. Some of this change has been desirable in the interest of efficient government but it has taken place in a manner which makes it difficult for Parliament to oversee. Hence the ease with which, in recent times, many undesirable changes have occurred. The ever-changing nature of the British Constitution makes any exact definition of the Prime Minister's power difficult. Yet it has been obvious in this century that even the pretence that the Prime Minister is *primus inter pares* has been impossible for any impartial observer to accept. His complete freedom of choice in determining the composition of the Cabinet assures him of a body of men who agree with him on all the essentials; while his large personal civil service puts at his disposal resources which are simply not available to his colleagues. At any one time the Prime Minister is the only member of the Cabinet who knows everything that is going on. Parliament, which knows much less than the meanest member of the Cabinet, becomes a backwater, incapable of creating anything more than a brief eddy. Labour survived the economic crisis of 1947 and the failure of British policy in Palestine, crises which would have brought down most nineteenth century governments. The Tories survived Suez to win an increased majority in 1959, and at one point in 1964 it looked as if they might even survive the disasters of their last two years in power. Both Eden and Macmillan resigned on account of ill-health; they could not otherwise have been removed. The truth is that within the present frame-work of Parliamentary procedure and party politics the machinery for dealing with such crises is inadequate. Government today is too complicated for effective checks to be possible without radical (as opposed to superficial) changes. 'Owing to the obsolete internal machinery of the House of Commons', wrote Beatrice and Sidney Webb in 1920, 'and to the immense variety and complexity of the issues with which it nowadays purports to deal, the power which it is incapable of exercising has been virtually transferred to the Prime Minister and his co-opted group of colleagues in the Cabinet and by them to the civil service acting in conjunction with powerful outside interests. The result is that under the guise of government by the majority of the people acting through its elected representatives, we now have the dictatorship of one man, or of a small group of men, exercised through a subservient party majority of more or less tied members, and an obedient official hierarchy of unparalleled magnitude.'[1] This description of the situation in 1920 exactly describes the parliamentary disease of 1968.

[1] *A Constitution For The Socialist Commonwealth of Great Britain.* London: Longmans, Green 1920.

CHAPTER IV

THE PARTY MACHINES

Writing sixty years ago Ostrogorski reached the pessimistic conclusion that the parliamentary system was unlikely to survive the creation of the mass party. Some forty years earlier Bagehot while defining the House of Commons as the repository of political power recognized the danger of constituency government.

In a previous chapter I have argued that the Westminster pattern of democracy has broken down. I defined the central problem as the power of the Prime Minister buttressed by the influence of the Civil Service and the party machine. The sickness from which our political system suffers can only be cured by a reappraisal and even a readjustment of the functions and powers of the Prime Minister in relation to Parliament, the party leaders in relation to their parties, and the parties in relation to Parliament.

The conflict which Ostrogorski prophesied between the mass party and the party in Parliament has in fact at different times occurred in all three political parties. Parties in a loose sense have always existed since the late seventeenth century, but originally they were divided by basic attitudes to fundamental ideas such as religion and the monarchy, rather than by specific policy defined by any organized method. They had no discipline and were for the most part simply an association of great families or of friends; for example, in the late eighteenth and nineteenth centuries members of the Derby family joined the Tory Party out of family tradition rather than political principle.

During the nineteenth century parties became formalised as a direct result of Parliamentary reform. The abolition of rotten boroughs and the introduction of the secret ballot meant that no magnate had any seat 'in his pocket' after the 1870s. Consequently the independent element in the House of Commons, composed of men of means rich enough to buy their own seats and therefore responsible to no one, disappeared.

More significantly, the vast increase in the size of the electorate after 1868 and 1885 made electioneering a more complex and also a more national affair.

The first party to adapt itself to these changing circumstances was the Tory Party. Indeed, the fact that the Liberals were never at ease with a mass organization was a contributory factor in their eventual downfall. Whether by accident or by design Disraeli, in the florid words of *The Times*, 'discerned in the inarticulate mass of the English populace the Conservative working man as the sculptor perceives the angel prisoned in a block of marble'. The titles of the first few pamphlets of the National Union show in what direction its thoughts were wandering: *The Conservative Working Man, Who are the real friends of the people?, Conservative Legislation for the Working Classes.*

The Conservative National Union was actually founded in November 1867 at a meeting of 'gentlemen and delegates' at the Freemasons' Tavern, London; it was presided over by John Gorst, who defined its object as being 'to consider by what particular organization we may make these Conservative principles effective among the masses'. In the words of H. C. Raikes such an organization was to be 'the handmaid of the party', not a body dictating policy to Conservative MPs. The National Union, which was born of this meeting did not at first excite great interest, the Conference of 1868 being attended by only seven people, including the committee.

The first meetings of the National Union discussed administration only. It was not till 1876 that politics were discussed and then only to pass a vote of confidence in the leadership. In 1885

E

it began to discuss current political issues in a suitably deferential manner. Nevertheless, the Union was a symptom of a more formal party system which was coming into being. 'In the conduct of public affairs', Disraeli told a deputation of the Union in 1878, 'there is nothing more precious than discipline.'

The impact of the National Union is difficult to assess. The striking Conservative victory of 1874 almost certainly owed a lot to it. There were active Conservative Associations in 65 of the 74 constituencies that were won from Radicals. Even Lord Salisbury, not an admirer of the new democracy, recognized in the end the role of the National Union.

The issue of whether the National Union was to dictate policy, the 'caucus control' predicted by Ostrogorski, was largely settled by two attempts of frustrated Tory leaders to use the National Union to defeat the official leadership on an issue of policy. In the 1880s Lord Randolph Churchill tried to use the National Union in his struggle for the leadership against Lord Salisbury. 'If, by judicious management, he could dominate (the Union) and endow it with new powers', wrote Balfour, 'it might effectively further his political ends.' Balfour also considered that Churchill dropped his campaign for 'Tory Democracy' as soon as he thought he might come to control the Parliamentary party, in which case he might find the National Union a hindrance.

On the second occasion, a role remarkably like Lord Randolph's was played by his son Winston Churchill. In 1934, three years after Churchill's resignation from the shadow Cabinet on the India issue, the National Union again became a battleground between the leadership and its rivals for control over policy. After an evasion of the issue in 1933, the matter was raised acrimoniously in 1934 when the leadership avoided defeat in the Central Council of the Union by only 23 votes. The question at stake was more than India; it was the role of the conference. 'There is only one force which can now save India for the Empire —the Conservative Party—and the heart of that party is this conference'.

The Conservative Party was the creation of a few great Tory magnates. The Parliamentary party created its own foundations, the mass movement. It was therefore inevitable perhaps that all effective power should ultimately remain with the Parliamentary party and not with the conference. The Parliamentary Labour Party, on the other hand, was the creation of a mass movement. Labour also had bitter disputes over the constitution of the party, though in their case those who stood for the power of the Conference, although finally unsuccessful in practice, had a much better case in theory.

The Labour Party had its origins in a loose association of Trades Unions with some intellectuals; its aim was to improve the material and legal standing of those whom it represented. In 1903 the Conference of the Labour Representation Committee decided to impose discipline on the Parliamentary Party; although this discipline was to be imposed by the Parliamentary Labour Party itself, all candidates were to 'abide by the decisions of the group in carrying out the aims of this Constitution or resign'. At the beginning of the century expulsion, quite apart from endangering the member's chance of being returned at the next election, meant withdrawal of the salary paid to him by the Labour Representation Committee at a time when MPs were not paid. Rapidly the danger of control by the mass movement appeared—in 1905 Ben Tillet proposed to subject the Parliamentary Labour Party to the dictates of the TUC. When the elections of 1906 increased the party representation to 29, it adopted its present title and elected its officers.

Thus formally launched, the Parliamentary Labour Party's status received its first major threat in 1907. At the conference of that year there were no less than seventeen resolutions put down 'giving the Parliamentary party definite instructions to introduce this or that', as Keir Hardie said. A counter-resolution that resolutions of the conference were opinions and not instructions caused acrimonious debate. This was followed by years of violent recrimination from Trades Union leaders, in particular Ben Tillet. Purely constitutional issues became ideological when the Great War raised the questions of wartime direction of labour and of pacifism. The party was completely divided on whether to join Asquith's coalition of 1915 and also on whether to leave Lloyd George's Government in 1918. As a result of these bickerings a new constitution was drawn up in 1918. This laid down that 'the work of the party shall be under the direction and control of the Party Conference', although a number of loopholes ensured that in practice the status of the Parliamentary Labour Party was not greatly altered. In future years the bark of the mass movement was to be very much worse than its bite.

Ever since the crystallization of the constitution after the Great War, the Labour Party, while fulfilling some of Ostrogorski's predictions when in opposition, has shown itself very much like the other two parties when in office. Even in opposition the influence of the Conference on the Parliamentary Labour Party was not always decisive. Demands made in 1931 for the nationalization of the joint stock banks were ignored altogether in Labour's election manifestoes. In office the Labour Party has had even more in common with the others. This was clearly shown by the complete defeat of the ILP which stood above all for the direction of its own Parliamentary party by the movement outside. Maxton, the leader of the ILP, in the words of *The Times*, 'as chairman of a socialist organization and member of a socialist party, refused to accept blindly every decision arrived at by the Cabinet'. The final collapse of the second Labour government was only one more illustration of the irrelevance of the mass party (and even of most of the Parliamentary Labour Party) to the conduct of a Labour Government. Before that, the Conference had protested in vain (in 1930) about 'the amount of time which is again to be allowed to Cabinet ministers'. After the fall, the Conference fulminated (again in vain) on the lack of safeguards against independent action by a Labour Government. Philip Snowden in his memoirs summarized the position in both major parties when he stated: 'My experience of Party Conferences has taught me to attach very little importance to their resolutions. Conferences will talk; let them talk. Governments, including Labour governments, dispose of Conference resolutions.'

In recent years the Labour Party parliamentary leadership was even more dramatically challenged at the Scarborough Conference in 1960 and was actually defeated on the issue of unilateral disarmament. The Liberal Assembly held several disorganized conferences during the 1950s culminating in the Assembly of 1958 on which *The Times* observed 'Lacking firm direction or guidance from the platform the Conference has gone from confusion to chaos'. Yet despite the great differences both in composition and powers between the parties' mass movements, the conflicts which have arisen between the Parliamentary leadership and the party conferences have resulted in ultimate victory for the leadership.

Though the composition and the powers of the National Party Movements vary widely their main objective is the same. This is to create a mass voluntary organization throughout the country and in each consistency with the aim of returning to Westminster the maximum number of Members of Parliament, in order to form a Government. It follows that in order to fulfil this aim and to attract sufficient national popular support a mechanism must exist for the leadership to hear the views and test the mood of the committed party workers and a platform must be provided for the unfolding of policies by the party leaders. Hence the development of the Annual Party Conference.

Of the three party conferences the function (in theory at least) of the Conservative Conference is the least precisely defined. It plays a purely advisory role in the formulation of policy; since its growth into a body of several thousand in the post-war period it has only once taken a vote on a controversial political issue where the outcome was in doubt.[1]

[1] At Brighton in October 1967 there was a vote at the end of the Education Debate when the officially supported motion was carried by 1302 to 816.

It is not in the least clear whether anybody is formally committed by a Conservative Party Conference vote and the Conservative leadership has never yet been defeated by a Conference vote. The most striking instance of the Conservative leadership being bulldozed into a policy commitment by the Conservative Conference was in 1950. Then the Conference insisted upon a target of 300,000 houses a year which Lord Woolton accepted with benign grace. But apart from Education in 1967 there have been only two issues of internal political controversy which have within contemporary political memory been both debated and voted upon at a Conservative Party Conference. These were the India policy in the 1930s and the question of Britain's entry into the Common Market in 1962. The narrow majority on the former issue I have already described; in 1962 with the enlarged Conference at Llandudno spread over three halls the Chairman felt sufficiently confident of the result to say by mistake 'We will take the amendment first and after that has been beaten we will vote on the main question'. His confidence was justified; only a handful of delegates voted against the leadership.

In 1965 at the Conservative Conference at Brighton the discussion on Rhodesia provided the only genuine debate, which was fiercely argued with real emotion. Paradoxically, although a solemn ritual of voting took place on every motion with at most three or four hands raised against the proposition, on the only motion that mattered in terms of controversy and where a decisive majority in favour of the platform would have been desirable standing orders were violated and a vote was avoided. Thus it was genuinely possible for Lord Salisbury to claim a considerable victory. For if he had not obtained his majority he had at least shaken the platform's nerve. I believe that this decision to avoid a vote was a cardinal error, as I said to Mr Heath and the Chairman of the Conference at the time. It gave encouragement to Mr Smith and his supporters in Salisbury; it showed, no doubt correctly, that the Conservative Party was split on the issue of sanctions against Rhodesia without bringing into the open the numerical strength on each side. It undoubtedly contributed towards the indecisive stand of the Conservative Party on the Rhodesia issue and adversely affected the Conservative fortunes in the General Election in March 1966. It is clear that the Conservatives must reform their conference procedure.

First, it is necessary to examine how the Chairman of the Conservative Conference comes to be presiding over a mass gathering of several thousand people. He is one of four officers of the National Union recommended for election to this post by the members of the Executive Committee of the National Union, all of whom hold office through holding other ex-officio posts, through co-option or through a process of indirect election. In theory the Chairman of the Party Conference, who is also Chairman of the National Union, can be opposed and the recommendation of the National Union Executive Committee can in fact be ignored. In practice this does not happen. The result is that each year the Conservative Conference is chaired by someone whose name and face are probably not known to more than a handful of delegates. He is seldom identified with any recognizable strand of Conservative thought. He needs, but rarely possesses, considerable political skill, as the 1965 Rhodesia debate all too clearly showed. The first need, therefore, is for the Chairman of the Conservative Conference to be directly elected by the delegates themselves. This would ensure that people with a genuine following would be chosen.

The second need is to reform the agenda of Conservative Conferences. Constituency Conservative Associations should be encouraged to put forward meaningful and even controversial resolutions to the Conference. This should be the responsibility of the Political Education Committee in each constituency, now always known as the C.P.C. Committee. Those who run the Conference should recognize that controversy and even voting does not necessarily indicate a damaging split, indeed the avoidance of a vote, as happened in the Rhodesia debate, can be even more damaging. A directly-elected Conference Management Committee might have the task of choosing the motions to be debated from among those submitted. I would not wish to see the voting results at Conservative Party Conferences binding the party leader in any future party policy statements, yet there must be a place for serious discussion if policy is to be framed through a two-way interchange of ideas.

If the Conservative Conference suffers from too little formalization the reverse is true of the Labour Party. Representation, two different forms of voting procedure, a show of hands and the card vote, and accountability are all clearly laid down. Controversy has always been the hallmark of the proceedings. An essential feature of the Labour Party Conference is that it contains representation both from Constituency Labour Parties and from affiliated Trade Unions. Each organization is entitled to be represented by one delegate for each five thousand members. Although the Trade Unions are normally heavily under-represented by delegates, when a card vote is called for their overwhelming voting strength is reflected. They then outnumber the Constituency Labour Party delegates by five to one. Until the recent past the Parliamentary leadership has managed to keep a measure of control over the Conference through an alliance with the leaders of certain key unions with large card votes to deliver. The real clash between the Parliamentary Party and the Conference arose in 1960 when the traditional co-operation between the massive Trade Unions and the leadership had broken down on the issue of unilateral disarmament, and after the accession of Frank Cousins to the General Secretaryship of the Transport and General Workers Union.

Until 1960 it had always been assumed that the Labour leadership was bound on a great issue of policy by a Conference vote; indeed Hugh Gaitskell confirmed that this was his interpretation of the situation in an interview in July 1959. However, when it was clear in 1960 that the leadership would in all likelihood be defeated on the unilateral issue, he announced in advance that in the event of an adverse vote he and his friends would 'fight and fight and fight again' to save the party they loved. This in fact he did and the following year the previous decision of the 1960 Labour Conference was defeated by an overwhelming majority. It has always in practice been clear that a Labour Government would not be bound by Conference votes, but until Gaitskell fought the Conference and won it was less clear that the Parliamentary Leadership when in Opposition would have a similar independence. Even on this occasion it was essential for the leadership to win the vote in 1961, since Gaitskell could obviously not have survived annual adverse votes on this or any other issue. Gaitskell's victory in 1961, made it possible for Harold Wilson to declare in 1963, on the day that he became Labour Party Leader, that he was not bound by the Conference decision passed in 1961 to demand the removal of the American Polaris submarine base from Britain.

In my view the Party Conferences of both the two major parties suffer from major defects. The Conservative Conference still too closely resembles a prize-giving ceremony. Its conduct is amateur, there is insufficient opportunity for debate, the authorities are frightened of openly-expressed dissenting views. As the party's greatest single annual exercise in public relations, in the presence of the television cameras and the press of the world, it is therefore a failure. The Labour Conference has defects which are in some ways even more serious. I have drawn attention to the power of the affiliated Trade Unions exercised through the card vote. The simple reason why the Labour leadership carried their vote in the 1954 Conference on German re-armament and lost their vote in 1960 on unilateral disarmament was that by 1960 Frank Cousins had replaced Arthur Deakin as the General Secretary of the most powerful Union. It is at least open to debate as to whether by a simple majority of votes the rank and file members of the Transport and General Workers' Union had, in this intervening period, changed their views so dramatically through transferring their support from someone as right wing as Arthur Deakin to someone as left wing as Frank Cousins. It is this manipulation of the card vote, sometimes through the influence of one man, which is the greatest single flaw in the Labour Party's democratic processes. Nor has the supremacy of Parliament over the mass membership yet been fully established in the Labour Party. Yet this assertion of authority is essential if the constitutional proprieties of parliamentary government are to be maintained. The Labour Conference is too formalized and the Conservative Conference too loosely organized. The votes at the Labour Conference are too susceptible to lobbying; at the Conservative Conference there are, as yet, no votes to be bought.

Party conferences happen only once a year, but both parties are sustained throughout the year by a professional party organization. In the Labour Party, Transport House is responsible to the National Executive Committee, which in turn is responsible to the party conference. The Conservative Central Office is the personal property of the leader of the party, its chief officers are appointed by him and are solely responsible to him. This situation more accurately reflects the party leader's status of bygone days. It would be right for the Conservative Central Office to be answerable to a strengthened National Executive composed of elected members from the party in Parliament and representatives of the mass membership of the party directly elected by the party conference. In this way the three organs of the Conservative Party—the Members of Parliament, the voluntary workers and the party machine—would be closely interrelated.

I have previously referred to the problems of the independently minded Member of Parliament. That such a person has a role is obvious; his ability to survive in present circumstances is more debatable. In the Labour Party his existence has hitherto been threatened by the oppressive application of the standing orders of the Parliamentary Labour Party. These involve the withdrawal of the whip if he votes against party decisions or even abstains, except on a clearly defined issue of conscience. The liberal regime instituted by Mr Richard Crossman and Mr John Silkin goes some way towards meeting the problem. In the Conservative Party oppressive discipline is in the main exerted by Constituency Conservative Associations. There has been no instance in the post-war period of the whip being withdrawn from a rebellious member, but several members were refused re-nomination by their Constituency Associations after Suez in 1956 and others have secured re-nomination only after a fight with their Constituency officers. It was possibly with this kind of danger in mind that Bagehot wrote: 'Constituency Government is the precise opposite of Parliamentary Government. It is the Government of immoderate persons far from the scene of action, instead of the Government of moderate persons close to the scene of action; it is the judgement of persons judging in the last resort and without a penalty, in lieu of persons judging in fear of a dissolution and ever conscious that they are subject to an appeal.' Though I favour the removal of the power of dissolution from the Prime Minister I have always been conscious of the power of dismissal by my electors as a whole, and it is to them that a Member of Parliament must ultimately be accountable.

Few aspiring Members of Parliament, in my experience, are so overwhelmed by the importance which they attach to this rank that they would willingly participate in a process that led to the replacement of parliamentary government by constituency government. Many present Conservative Members of Parliament are aware of the dangers which peculiarly exist in the Conservative Party today. It is because I am aware of this danger, which to a minor extent I have encountered, that I am determined to fight it from Westminster.

CHAPTER V

THE PRIME MINISTER AND THE PRESIDENT

It is often claimed that today the Prime Minister has presidential powers, and that a General Election is more in the nature of a presidential campaign than a choice between competing parties. This comparison is heightened by the suggestion that Mr Wilson has modelled himself on the late President Kennedy, and by the allusive title of the book *The Making of a Prime Minister*.[1]

Direct comparison between the two offices is easily clouded by the disproportionate difference in the degree of real power wielded by each in terms of world influence.

But a careful analysis of the roles of the two leaders shows that the British Prime Minister is considerably more powerful in his own sphere than his American counterpart is in his. Like a President, the Prime Minister possesses extensive powers of patronage. He also has the power to appoint and dismiss Ministers; appointments, in the case of the President, are subject to confirmation by Congress. In addition the Prime Minister has in his armoury the powerful weapon of dissolution of Parliament, and exercises control and supervision of the party machines.

On the other hand, the President has a fixed term of office (four years), whereas the Prime Minister's tenure of office is dependent on retaining the support of a majority in the House of Commons.

It is doubtful if an allusion of presidential powers would have

[1] Anthony Howard and Richard West, Jonathan Cape (1965).

been made of the British Prime Minister at the beginning of this century. That such a comparison can now be made without raising the eyebrows of more than a few constitutional historians is indicative of the considerable political developments which have occurred in the last fifty years. The process of acquisition of executive powers in the hands of one man—begun by Lloyd George in 1916, accelerated by Churchill in the second world war and in Harold Macmillan's seven-year term—has been completed by Harold Wilson. This process has been spasmodic, at times barely perceptible—but inevitable. It has owed much to the life and death struggles of two world wars, and to the economic crises which followed them.

As recently as 1933, Professor D. W. Brogan was saying in his book *The American Political System*: 'No matter how great the authority of an English Prime Minister, he is not yet the complete master of the situation as is the President (of the United States).' 'The President is no mere *primus inter pares*', said Brogan, tacitly subscribing to the traditional view of the Prime Minister's role in England. But a present-day assessment leads one to a different conclusion; that the powers, as well as the authority, of a British Prime Minister enable him to establish an ascendancy over his colleagues in the Cabinet which is unchallengeable.

Of course, no Prime Minister is unseatable, even between elections. Asquith was deposed in 1916 by a Cabinet move. Chamberlain resigned in 1940 after a vote of confidence in which thirty-five Government supporters defected to the opposition and sixty others abstained. The voting on the Government's handling of the Profumo affair in effect placed a time limit on the duration in office of Macmillan. Two of my former colleagues in Parliament told me that they were persuaded by the Whips to vote for the Government at the conclusion of the Profumo debate on the assurance that Mr Macmillan would have retired from the premiership by the Autumn.

In this respect, it can be argued that a Prime Minister is

somewhat more vulnerable than a President, who has a fixed term of office. During his four year term, a President is irremovable 'except on impeachment for and conviction of treason, bribery, or other high crimes and misdemeanours'.[1] Only once has Congress invoked this extreme remedy and then unsuccessfully.[2]

By comparison, a British Prime Minister appears more insecure, and can always be reminded that he exists in office by the licence of his supporters who form the majority in the House of Commons. Members of Parliament likewise wish to continue in office, and in keeping a weather eye open for their chances at the next election, they judge their leader's fortunes by his popularity with the electorate. The popular impact of a Prime Minister, his Government and its policies, can be assessed from time to time by means of public opinion polls and by-election results. A similar test applies in opposition. In 1965 the steady decline in support for Sir Alec Douglas-Home recorded by the opinion polls prompted a change in the leadership of the Conservative Party. An opposition leader is, however, more easily removed than a Prime Minister and it is doubtful whether Sir Alec would have resigned so promptly had he still been Prime Minister. In March 1962 the shock result of the Orpington by-election administered a sharp rebuff to the image of 'Super Mac', though he did not in fact resign.

And yet although on occasion a Prime Minister might echo the words of Richard III: 'Uneasy lies the head that wears a crown', nevertheless, provided that his nerve does not let him down in critical periods, he is in a strong position not only to control events but to influence public reaction to them. The importance of the Prime Minister's nerve is borne out by Lord Kilmuir's account in *Political Adventure* of his final interviews with Mr Macmillan after having been dismissed: 'I got the impression that he was extremely alarmed about his own position

[1] U.S. Constitution, Article II, Section 4.
[2] Against President Andrew Johnson, who was impeached in 1867.

and was determined to eliminate any risk for himself by a massive change of Government. It astonished me that a man who had kept his head under the most severe stresses should lose both his nerve and judgement in this way.'

Until 1916 the Prime Minister's personal staff was limited to a small number of private secretaries. This is still formally the position but the replacement of Cabinet rule by disguised Presidential rule dates from the creation of the Cabinet office by Lloyd George during the First World War. Although the intention was to service and give reality to a formal constitutional entity, in practice the Cabinet office, formed during the First World War and vastly expanded during the Second, has become the servant of the Prime Minister who presides over the Cabinet.

Armed with a secretariat it was possible for the Prime Minister to formulate policy and take decisions without consulting, or even informing, the Cabinet as a whole. The resolve to manufacture atomic weapons was never formally put to the Cabinet and the plans for the Suez operation were put to the Cabinet only four days before the Israeli attack. In these two instances the role of the Cabinet was not dissimilar from the habitual role of the House of Commons, namely to rubber stamp a decision which had already been taken and which could not be reversed.

While the combined staff of the Cabinet office and that of Number 10 Downing Street is small compared with that attached to the White House and although there is nothing to compare with the quasi-political presidential assistants who frequently have more influence than American Cabinet members, the Prime Minister now has a presidential staff at his command.

In his dealings with his parliamentary party the Prime Minister wields the powerful weapon of patronage either in the form of ministerial appointments or political honours,[1] which deters many career-conscious MPs from indulging in the unrewarding luxury

---

[1] The Labour Party says that it does not now give political honours (Prime Minister's statement to Parliament October 27th, 1966). However, honours for political services are still given to worthy aldermen which one suspects are disguised political honours.

of revolt. Furthermore, he can hold over the heads of critical backbenchers the sanction of dissolution of Parliament. The threat to dissolve Parliament was specifically made by Mr Wilson to a meeting of the Parliamentary Labour Party on March 2, 1967, when castigating those who had abstained from voting in support of the Government's defence policy. The making of such a threat for disciplinary purposes less than a year from the beginning of a Parliament containing a Government majority of nearly a hundred is without precedent and gives added point to the powerlessness of Parliament as a check on the Executive.

Finally, and most importantly, the Prime Minister has effective control of the party machines which could enable him to mobilize support in the constituencies against any attempt by the Parliamentary Party to unseat him. Mr Wilson's warning on March 2, 1967, to the rebellious member, 'He may not get his [dog] licence renewed when it falls due', indicates the power of the party machine in the nomination of candidates for Parliament.

With all these weapons at his disposal a Prime Minister can take on most of the challenges to his tenure and emerge victorious.

For instance, Attlee, despite having the largest-ever Labour majority in the Commons, was faced in 1947 with a Cabinet conspiracy to replace him by Bevin. He successfully turned the flank of the conspirators by appointing Cripps (the prime malcontent) to a new Ministry of Economic Affairs, and shortly afterwards (following Dalton's indiscretion) to the Exchequer.

This power of appointment and of dismissal of Ministers is the key to the Prime Minister's ascendancy over his Cabinet colleagues. Whereas a Prime Minister can be got rid of only with difficulty, as a result of what Richard Crossman describes as 'a coup d'état', a Cabinet Minister can be dismissed summarily— and not merely for incompetence, dereliction of his duties or scandalous behaviour, but at the whim of his appointer.

Many are the stories, true or false, of ministers reading for the first time in the morning papers the news that they had resigned the previous evening. As one of Trollope's characters exclaimed, 'It seemed to me but the other day that everybody connected with the government was living in fear lest he should resign'.

The Prime Minister's discretion in forming his Cabinet is limited only by certain very broad axioms of political prudence. Ramsay Muir, whose book, *How Britain is Governed*, was one of the many strong protests at constitutional developments which appeared during the 1930s, wrote—'The Cabinet is in short the steering wheel of the ship of state. But the steersman is the Prime Minister. He not only assigns them to their offices, he can dismiss any of them or transfer them from one office to another; and within certain limits he can determine the size of the Cabinet. . . .' The freedom of the Prime Minister in making appointments was fully demonstrated by Baldwin, who offered the Exchequer in 1923 to a Liberal (McKenna) in place of a Tory (Horne) who had expected to retain it, and in 1924 to Churchill, who had been elected as a Constitutionalist and did not in fact become a Conservative till the following year.

Dismissals are in theory the prerogative of the Queen. It is still the pure constitutional theory that each minister is responsible on his own account to the Monarch who can dismiss each in turn. In the eighteenth century, when this actually happened, it created an important ceiling to the Prime Minister's power. In the nineteenth century it ceased to happen, the power being transferred to the Prime Minister. The Prime Minister was compelled then, however, to pay regard to the wishes of Parliament, especially since in that age of personality politics many Cabinet ministers (Cobden and Bright, or Huskisson, for instance) would have an important Parliamentary following in their own right. Gladstone had strong doubts on a Prime Minister's right to dismiss Ministers, regarding them, as Sir William Harcourt wrote, as being 'to a great degree autonomous in their own province'. In 1880, when Gladstone asked Lord Carrington to resign, the latter refused and Gladstone, unsure of his powers, dropped his action for a year. Nevertheless, Pitt secured the dismissal of a troublesome Lord Chancellor as early as 1792. In 1851, Lord Russell very obviously and publicly dismissed Lord Palmerston who had without any authority from the Cabinet congratulated Louis Napoleon on his successful *coup d'état* in France—though here Russell was enthusiastically supported by the Queen. Palmerston himself declared that the Prime Minister had a right to 'remove any members of the government whom he may think it is better to remove than to retain in the Cabinet'. Even at that time, however, the Queen retained less power over appointments than she imagined: she stood out against the appointment of Sir Charles Dilke to the Cabinet (on personal rather than political grounds—he had been involved in a divorce scandal), but her stand was in any case convenient for the rest of the Cabinet who found Dilke's earnest enthusiasm a bore. Few dismissals could have been more arbitrary than Balfour's of 1903, when Lord George Hamilton (one of those who resigned) said, 'A Prime Minister has an undoubted right to request any of his colleagues, whose presence in the Cabinet is in his opinion or judgement prejudicial to the efficiency or policy of the government, to resign his office'[1]; which firmly established the principle that a Prime Minister can dismiss any minister not only for inefficient deeds but also for unacceptable words. Equally a Prime Minister can and does demote or transfer a troublesome minister. In 1917 Lloyd George removed Carson from the position of First Lord of the Admiralty to Minister without Portfolio. In 1948, after the economic crisis, Shinwell was transferred from the Ministry of Fuel and Power to the non-Cabinet position of War Minister. As recently as January 1967 Fred Lee and Arthur Bottomley, whilstre maining in the Government, were dropped from the Cabinet.

But the Prime Minister's right to determine the composition of his Cabinet received its most dramatic unveiling in July 1962, when Macmillan dismissed a third of his Cabinet at one stroke. Seven went: Selwyn Lloyd (Chancellor of the Exchequer), Hill

[1] Quoted in Hobhouse *Life of the Duke of Devonshire.*

(Housing), Maclay (Scotland), Eccles (Education), Mills (Minister without Portfolio), Kilmuir (Lord Chancellor), and Watkinson (Defence). This 'Cabinet massacre' coincided with the Leicester N.E. by-election and was designed to infuse fresh young blood into the Government. The brutal haste of the dismissals is revealed in the memoirs of Lord Hill of Luton: 'I had no reason to complain of his decision until I learned that the changes were to be announced at seven that evening. That seemed to me to be precipitately hasty as well as personally embarrassing.' 'A good Prime Minister', Hill went on to comment, 'ought not to risk the charge that he destroyed others in order to save himself.' But the decision, although having a catastrophic effect on Conservative morale—the reverse of what was intended—, was accepted as being within the Prime Minister's prerogative.

By contrast, an American President is limited to recommending appointments to Congress for approval, even though members of the Cabinet are members of his staff with no formal accountability to Congress. In most cases this amounts to a mere formality, but the difficulties which can face a controversial appointment are dramatically portrayed in Allen Drury's novel *Advise and Consent*. There was a long-drawn-out conflict in 1887 between President Hayes and the Senate over two of the appointments he wished to make to his Cabinet.[1]

However, once appointed, British Cabinet Ministers are accountable to Parliament for their actions which, where necessary, they defend in Parliament. Under the doctrine of Ministerial responsibility to Parliament, a vote of censure on an individual Minister in the Commons would result in his resignation. In the American Cabinet members who cannot be members of Congress are responsible to the President and, although their actions can be reviewed by Congressional Committees, they cannot be restricted in the exercise of their executive functions.

Perhaps the most important difference in the offices of Prime Minister and President is the power to dissolve Parliament. In

[1] The appointments were those of David M. Key and Carl Schurz.

theory it lies with the whole Cabinet to recommend to the sovereign that Parliament should be dissolved and a General Election held. In practice this decision devolves on the Prime Minister.

It is axiomatic that the right to dissolve Parliament will be used to favour the party in power.[1] As a consequence of being able to choose the most favourable electoral opportunity to hold an election, the Conservatives were able to increase their majorities in 1955 and 1959 and only narrowly suffered defeat in 1964. The same tactic was skilfully employed by Harold Wilson in March 1966, prior to the unpopular July measures of the same year (although he could convincingly plead in this case for the need to establish a working majority). Constitutionally this power owed its origin and justification to the period when the Commons was a militant body and opposed legislation which was controversial. If the Government was sufficiently determined to press through with legislation, it had to go to the country for a mandate. Frustration of the Government's legislative programme by the Upper House was the reason why Asquith felt compelled in 1910 to call an election and ask for a popular mandate to reform the House of Lords. The growth of the party machine in the Commons and the curtailment of the Lords' power to delay legislation has removed much of the necessity for this weapon. But its usefulness to the Government is now assessed in terms of electoral advantage.

The American system is less susceptible to electoral manipulation. Every four years the President must either present himself to the electorate for re-election or, if he has been in office for two full consecutive terms, retire. Similarly Congress is subject to fixed elections: every even-numbered year the whole House of Representatives and a third of the Senate must face an election. The American system, therefore, provides a measure of continuity both in Government and in legislative membership.

[1] While this has not always worked in the past, e.g. Gladstone attempted an unheralded snap election in 1874 and was defeated and a similar fate overtook Baldwin in 1923, the greatly increased ability of Government to manipulate the economy in the post 1945 period has made Governments increasingly difficult to defeat.

Party discipline in the United States is much less rigid. Congress can, and frequently does, ignore the party (or presidential) line and vote as it thinks fit. In this respect, it is a much more independent assembly than the House of Commons because the views of the electorate (with wider local variations) and of the individual Senator or Congressman are held in greater account than strict adherence to the party whip. Consequently, the passing of Government legislation cannot be regarded as automatic. Something like half the Bills which the United States Administration asks for do not get passed. This is true even when the Administration has a majority in Congress, as in the case of Kennedy, who failed to get through his Civil Rights legislation and other radical measures. But the difficulty of legislating is compounded when the majority in either House of Congress is of a different political persuasion from the President, a situation that cannot exist in the British parliamentary system. In these circumstances, where the legislative programme of the Administration can be blocked by opposing forces in Congress, the principal disadvantage of this form of separation of powers is displayed.

The opportunities for frustration of positive action have at times produced a cynical assessment of the worth of American institutions. Bagehot wrote: 'The English Constitution, in a word, is framed on the principle of choosing a single, sovereign authority, and making it good; the American, on the principle of having many sovereign authorities, and hoping that their multitude may atone for their infirmity.'

The danger of legislative impotence has been removed from the British scene by the imposition of the whipping system into Parliament. The strict control of discipline is backed by the rewards of office for good behaviour and the ultimate sanction of expulsion from the party. A British Prime Minister, therefore, has a clear advantage over a President in the legislative, as opposed to the executive, sphere of government. He is assured of majority support in the House of Commons; and, by the twin methods of rewarding and cajoling used by the whips, he can invariably get through Parliament even unpopular measures. The prime example of this is the prices and incomes legislation, which received a stormy passage in debate at the hands of Government backbenchers, but was nevertheless undefeated. It is inconceivable that a similarly controversial measure could have been piloted successfully through a hostile Congress with so little difficulty in so short a time.

Successive British Prime Ministers have made the domestic position of the Prime Minister immeasurably more potent than that of the American President. In the nineteenth century Bagehot allowed himself to think that the efficient part of Parliament's duties was to elect the Prime Minister and the Cabinet, in deference to the theory that no man could become Prime Minister unless he could command sufficient parliamentary support. The party machine has removed the need for parliamentary consultation.

The decision as to who will be Prime Minister is taken by the electorate on polling day, without reference either to Parliament or even to those Members of Parliament who belong to the Party with a majority in the House of Commons. They could only come into their own if an existing Prime Minister were to retire in advance of a General Election. When this has happened in the past, under periods of Conservative rule, the decision as to a successor has been taken by the Cabinet, except in 1963 when the process, which was anything but customary, most closely resembled an American party convention without the votes.

It is perhaps unrealistic to expect a greater measure of parliamentary control over the choice of the Prime Minister. Indeed, the Conservative Party made a distinct advance in constitutional propriety when it decided to follow the Labour Party in securing the election of its leader by the members of the parliamentary party. But the fact remains that it is extremely difficult to dispose of a party leader, let alone a Prime Minister. Mr Harold Wilson was originally elected leader of the Labour Party by a body that bears little resemblance to the present Parliamentary Labour Party. The annual ritual of his unopposed re-election has little meaning. Unlike the American President who has under the Constitution a fixed term of office, a British Prime Minister can be removed only at a General Election at a timing of his own choice, or be de-stooled like an African tribal chief.

Those who think that British Constitutional reform is basically about parliamentary procedure are attacking the problem at the circumference; the central problem is about the power of the Prime Minister. I accept that we are now operating a presidential system; to do otherwise would be unrealistic. Let us concede the Prime Minister presidential powers and equip ourselves with the necessary safeguards.

CHAPTER VI

PARLIAMENT AND COMMITTEES

At the time of writing *The English Constitution*, Bagehot was largely justified in describing the House of Commons as one of the efficient elements of the constitution, but (as Richard Crossman has written) 'this has now become part of the constitutional myth'. As far back as 1931 Lloyd George told the Select Committee on Procedure that 'Parliament has really no control over the executive. It is pure fiction.'

The decline in the power of Parliament has been caused by the emergence of the party machines and the intensification of party discipline, the increasing importance first of the Cabinet and later of the Prime Minister, the complexity of modern government and the consequent growth in the Civil Service, and the absence of any effective parliamentary machinery for scrutiny or checking.

The function of Parliament was analysed by J. S. Mill as 'to watch and control the Government; to throw the light of publicity on its acts; to compel a full exposition and justification of all of them which anyone considers questionable; to censure them if found condemnable, and if the men who compose the Government abuse their trust or fulfil it in a manner which conflicts with the deliberate sense of the nation to expel them from office, and either expressly or virtually appoint their successors. This is surely ample power and security enough for the liberty of the Nation.' Scarcely one of these functions is carried out today.

The Executive has either been content to watch the traditional powers of Parliament fall into disuse, or actually been instrumental in accelerating this process. To quote Hans Daalder in *Cabinet Reform in Britain 1914–1963*: 'The House of Commons has become an arena for public debate between the Government and the opposition rather than a distinct organ of legislation and control.' Richard Crossman, the only leading politician in the last half century to have expressed any genuine concern about the status and functions of Parliament before himself becoming the Leader of the House of Commons, revealed his awareness of the problem in his introductory analysis of Bagehot's work: he concluded that 'the Commons has lost its collective will and finally become the forum of debate between well-disciplined political armies'.

Paradoxically, just as at the time when Bagehot was writing the House of Commons was already being transformed into one of the dignified parts of the constitution, so is Crossman's analysis ceasing to be valid. For the House of Commons is no longer the main battleground between the great political parties. The real contest is waged between the rival efficiencies of the party machines and through the mass media of communications. Even inside Parliament discussion of controversial issues often takes place at formal private meetings of party committees.[1] Formal parliamentary debate is a mock contest, designed neither to repel nor persuade, conducted with ritualistic favour to its futile and inevitable conclusion.

Any Government which has a majority, however small, can carry its legislative programme through Parliament in spite of all the efforts of the Opposition. This was clearly demonstrated by the Labour Government which came to power in October

---

[1] Private meetings must have gone on as long as politics have been politics. Gladstone's supporters used to meet in the Tea Room in the House to discuss their line on the Reform Bill in 1867. The real danger which exists today is that these meetings acquire the power of a caucus and enforce Policy before debate.

1964 with a majority of five (soon to be reduced to three) and which remained in power for eighteen months through the efficient operation of the Government Whips. That Government went so far in the winter of 1965 when sickness jeopardized its majority as to threaten to introduce proxy voting into the House if the opposition whips did not provide alternative acceptable pairing methods, actually going to the point of pairing non-sick Conservatives with sick Socialists. The traditional function of the Opposition has been to check the excesses of the Government, but the strict manipulation through the Government Whips of a majority in the House of Commons has reduced the role of the Opposition to one of mere protest.

Such curbing of the Executive which now remains has passed from the Opposition to the Government backbenchers. It is instigated by dissatisfaction with Government policy and is vented through abstention and, more rarely, opposing votes, and through backbench party committee criticisms. It is obviously conditioned by the size of the Government majority in the House of Commons. Overt criticism of Mr Wilson's first Government was stifled by the narrow majority, but the landslide in 1966 provided scope for Government backbenchers to express their individual dissent from Mr Wilson's policies on prices and incomes, foreign policy (Vietnam and Aden), defence and the Common Market. While Crossman is broadly correct in saying that 'Once the party leadership has a modern machine and can discipline its MPs, Government control of Parliament and its business becomes absolute', it is also paradoxically true that the larger a parliamentary majority the greater is the chance of effecting a change in Government policy through parliamentary pressure. To quote Ronald Butt, the political correspondent of *The Financial Times*, 'So far as determining or limiting the action of a Government is concerned, only the majority is decisive and as long as the Government can hold its party together the Opposition is impotent except to influence public debate in preparation for the next General Election'. The withdrawal in the spring of

1967 of the more extreme proposals to back the proposed system of voluntary restraint on incomes and the reduction of the delaying power of the Prices and Incomes Board from twelve months to six months are clear examples of a retreat in favour of Government back bench opinion.

A further development has been the tendency to debate and discuss issues of controversy in advance and in private within the party parliamentary committees. A case in point was the Labour Government's controversial decision to implement the change-over to decimal currency on the £ (rather than the 10s.) unit. The Government decided to debate the matter beforehand in party committee and to resolve there the question of obedience to the Government line. No measure was more obviously suited to non-party discussion and a free vote of Parliament. Yet for reasons of administrative speed and convenience the Government opted to impose a three-line Whip in the debate and force through its views despite substantial opposition both inside and outside Parliament. Justification was offered for the Government's attitude by a Labour MP, Mr R. B. Cant, who declared in a letter to *The Financial Times*, 'This is a country that has opted for strong Government and in that context the democratic checks and balances exist not on the floor of the House of Commons, but in pre-legislative consultation'. Not only was this episode dubious in its constitutional antecedents, but it exposed the absurdity and futility of formal opposition and marked a dangerous advance in removing Parliamentary decision-making from the floor of the House.

Another example of the increasing importance attached to influencing back bench opinion within the milieu of the Party Committee rather than on the floor of the House was the series of meetings held by the Parliamentary Labour Party on the Common Market issue following the visits of Mr Wilson and Mr Brown to the European capitals in the spring of 1967. Mr Wilson cannot be wholly blamed for holding the meetings which were a recognition of the need to present as united a front as possible when the issue was presented for public debate. But the nature of the meetings was something new. Mr Wilson said that he thought that the information which he and Mr Brown had collected on their European tour 'shouldn't only be confined to the Cabinet' it should also be made available to the 'majority party', and Mr Wilson added that he was happy to make all the information available to the Opposition so that they could have party meetings on it too. The normal practice for a Government is to issue information to Parliament in the form of a White Paper which can then be debated. The issuing of Government Information to party committees which are merely unofficial groups of ambiguous constitutional standing is detrimental to Parliament, since it encourages the leaders on both sides to talk each to their own followers with neither side really giving precedence to the debate across the floor.

These developments must cause serious concern to any constitutional lawyer. One of the most eminent of them, Sir Ivor Jennings, has said 'Freedom of debate in Parliament is one of the most important political principles'. This freedom is now challenged by a rigid whipping system which allows little scope for individual consciences, and by a growing tendency of the Government to refer matters to the Parliamentary Labour Party in advance of Parliament itself after they have already been irrevocably decided in Cabinet. Today the Executive reigns supreme, but as Jennings points out 'it is in Parliament that the focus of our liberties must be found'.

If Parliament has now become inadequate even as a debating forum, its capability to bridle the power of the Executive appears even more folorn, particularly when compared with the powers of the United States Congress. In the United States scrutiny is in the hands of Standing Committees of Congress; in 1950-51 Congress authorized the expenditure of 7·6 million dollars for such investigations. Dr W. H. Brubeck has estimated (colloquium on the Committee System, London June 24, 1967) that between $20 and $30 million, or about 1/10 of the budget of

Congress, is allocated to the work of the Committees of Congress. In the field of delegated legislation Government agencies must make regular reports to Congress which may demand any files and withdraw or limit any delegated power; in the sphere of spending Congress has rigid powers of appropriation; treaties with foreign powers need to be ratified by a two-thirds majority of the Senate. Congress can regulate commerce, control immigration and declare war.

The House of Commons has no comparable authority. Its existing weapons against the Executive are fourfold. These are question time, Opposition supply days, the Scrutiny Committee on delegated legislation, and the Committees on Estimates and Public Accounts.

Question time in the House of Commons is not the searching inquisition that it is claimed to be. According to Hans Daalder, 'the introduction of the rota system in question time has had the effect of lessening ministerial answerability for a considerable number of ministers'. For example, questions to the Foreign Secretary are now reached about once in every five or six weeks. This lessening of answerability has occurred despite the fact that the extension of Government powers has increased the number of issues on which Ministers can technically be challenged in Parliament. To make matters worse, oral questions have become increasingly a political game in which the ability to score debating points is esteemed more highly than the quest for knowledge and information. Written questions are an even less satisfactory method of eliciting information from Ministers, when it is borne in mind that the answers are prepared by Civil Servants who have a vested interest in protecting their Minister or concealing their own mistakes and failures. In my personal experience the backbencher at question time is at the mercy of the Government department, which has all the information while he has little. His ability to probe is confined to two oral questions and two supplementary questions on each day that a particular departmental minister is answering. If his question is far down on the order paper it will not even be reached. Government departments do not hesitate to stonewall or evade. It may therefore take the persistent Member of Parliament three or four months to get to the bottom of a particular problem, if he manages to do so at all.

Since the war there has been an enormous growth in the amount of delegated legislation. In 1952, for example, 2,312 statutory instruments were registered under this heading. Theoretically the Scrutiny Committee of the House of Commons is responsible for the overall surveillance of this field of legislation. But the prolix and technical nature of this legislation inhibits serious and effective examination. In the words of Sir Cecil Carr 'Parliamentary control has in effect disappeared when with the aid of a substantial majority, the Government has secured the enactment of the parent statute, the opposition side has little hope of success in moving a motion for the annulment of the resultant statutory instrument'.

In any given session there are approximately twenty-six supply days in which the Opposition is traditionally allowed to debate a subject of its own choosing. Paradoxically this customary procedure has the effect of actually diminishing the amount of parliamentary control over the Executive. For its effect is to allow the voting of huge sums to Government departments to be taken on the nod and without debate so that the Opposition can debate a general subject of its choice when its chances of altering Government policy are, as we have seen, negligible.

There remain the Public Accounts and Estimates Committees, which exercise the important function of reviewing the financial administration of the Government. The Public Accounts Committee, which is serviced by the Comptroller and Auditor-General and is always under the chairmanship of a prominent opposition MP, has wide powers of investigation and has succeeded in unearthing a number of Government blunders, including the Ferranti affair. However, the fact that it operates so far in arrear of the events that it is investigating detracts from the effectiveness and immediacy of its reports, and gives it the inevitable role of uncovering scandals rather than that of determining policy. The Estimates Committee directs a searching eye from time to time on the work of individual Government departments. It is impeded in this task, since it is concerned with economy of expenditure rather than questioning of policy, and can rarely deal with more than one department at a time. Hence ten or more years may elapse before it takes a second look at a recommendation which it has made. Nevertheless it is true to say that these two Committees exemplify in a very limited way the processes by which the House of Commons could still fulfil its traditional role of checking the actions of the Executive.

Yet another sphere in which Congress has a clear advantage over Parliament is its power of investigation. The first Congressional enquiry was held in 1792, into the defeat of General St Clair by the Indians. More recently, in 1951–52, in one session Congress authorised 256 enquiries whose functions included the exposure of scandals, the scrutinizing of elections, a watch on pressure groups and assisting in impeachments. It is significant, by contrast, that the British Government did not choose a select committee of Parliament to deal with the Bristol Siddeley affair or to enquire into the Torrey Canyon incident, which was not a party political matter in any ordinary sense at all. The previous Conservative Government preferred to use the services of Lord Denning for the purpose of conducting an enquiry into the Profumo scandal and its aftermath. The Lynskey and Radcliffe Tribunals dealing with the Sidney Stanley episode and the alleged Bank Rate leak were other methods employed to bypass Parliament. The Committee of Privy Councillors on the D notice controversy, though not strictly a Parliamentary enquiry, was more parliamentary than a tribunal of enquiry would have been, but the results of their investigations were torn up. In the United States all these matters would have been investigated by Congress.

It is frequently supposed that many of the ills of the Westminster system could be cured by a more elaborate committee system. This requires further definition. The party committees, to which previous reference has been made, can best be disposed of by saying that they are not committees in any accepted parliamentary sense at all. Their membership is open to any MP of the political party concerned. If a matter of immediate interest and controversy is being discussed a particular meeting will be crowded out, at other times it might consist of only a handful of members. Meetings of party committees are simply private gatherings of a party caucus, often to decide the party line in advance, sometimes to hear a talk from an outside expert, but seldom to scrutinize a particular piece of legislation in detail,[1] still less to assert the rights of Parliament against the Executive. This is not to say that such meetings are in any way unnecessary or harmful, but simply that they are irrelevant to the strengthening of parliamentary institutions.

A category of committee which has a clearly defined role is the Standing Committee, which takes the committee stage of every Bill which is not taken on the floor of the House of Commons. Such a committee, which usually consists of fifty MPs drawn in proportion to party strengths in the House of Commons, is called together at the start of the committee stage of a Bill and is discharged when this has been completed. Unless the guillotine procedure is invoked, the Committee would discuss the Bill clause by clause. Because the whip operates in committee, it is unlikely (but not unknown) that any clause would be defeated or amendment accepted in a Government Bill without Government approval. The weakness of this form of committee procedure is that members are drafted on to committees at random, and they may have no experience or special knowledge of the Bill under discussion. The Committee stage of a Bill is conducted

---

[1] The Conservative Party Finance Committee in opposition has done a good deal of work on budget amendments but of course this Committee has nothing like the powers and equipment of Congress Committees.

according to a strict timetable. When a particular Committee has been discharged the knowledge that an MP may have acquired in a specialized field may never be put to use again. It is hardly surprising that Standing Committees, which are in effect no more than the House of Commons sitting in miniature, have little influence on Government policy. A Select Committee on Nationalized Industries was set up under the Conservative Government and has had limited success. More recently, as an experiment, two Select Committees of the House of Commons have been appointed to study agriculture, and science and technology. A Select Committee on the Parliamentary Commissioner is proposed to be appointed soon. It remains to be seen whether they will be effective in restoring authority to Parliament; on the whole this seems doubtful, since their scope is too limited.

I advocate the appointment of Select Committees on all the important areas of Government activity, such as external affairs, defence, economic affairs, education, social services, Home Office affairs, agriculture, and science and technology. I envisage that each committee would be served by a considerably expanded department under the Comptroller and Auditor-General. The committees would be manned in accordance with the respective representation of the parties in Parliament. The members would be elected by the backbenchers of each party and not appointed by the Whips. They would have the power both to scrutinize the administration of the relevant Government Departments and to question decisions of policy. They would be empowered to summon Ministers, Civil Servants, and the necessary papers. They would normally sit in public, but could elect to hear proceedings in camera, if security interests demanded this.

I further advocate that these specialist Select Committees would also assume the functions of the present Standing Committees. As such, the Committee stage of every Parliamentary Bill would have to be taken by the relevant specialist committee. This would mean that detailed scrutiny of all legislation would be allotted to a committee fully conversant with the affairs of the relevant Government department.

This would represent a major change in Parliamentary practice. For, as Herbert Morrison has said in *Government and Parliament*, 'Broadly speaking the function of examining and challenging important Government policy is reserved to Parliament as a whole. In the United States and France things are very different. . . . Budgets and legislation are exhaustively examined in Committees of the United States Congress and the French Parliament, which would often appear to have even more decisive powers and influence than the Parliamentary institution as a whole.' It is my conviction that Parliament as a whole is no longer able to fulfil the functions of examining and challenging important Government decisions. It can be argued that my proposals will shift control of the Executive from the Chamber of the House of Commons to the Committee room. I accept the force of that argument, but this is an inevitable and necessary development. The important need is to repatriate a measure of power from Whitehall to Westminster. This is the only way in which it can be done.

Professor D. W. Brogan has written of the United States Congress in *Parliament, a Survey*: 'If we wish to see the real masters of national politics, the equals of our front-bench men, we shall look for them not in the Cabinet Room, but in the Senate, a body which attracts the really vigorous and powerful figures in national politics.' If power were genuinely shared between Whitehall and Westminster, the same might be true of the non-ministerial Committee chairmen in Parliament.

CHAPTER VII

THE BACKBENCHER

The increase in the personal power of the Prime Minister, the devaluation of the Cabinet, the growing influence of the Civil Service and the creation of the party machines have all had the effect of diminishing the influence of the legislature and restricting the role of the Member of Parliament. He is the principal victim of the parliamentary disease. He is too much intimidated by Whips, over-pressurized by his party organizations and wholly dependent on the executive's will for his tenure of office.

The late Walter Elliot described Sir Alan Herbert, former independent Member for Oxford University, as 'a survival, even a throwback. He is the Member of Parliament such as nine-tenths were and not more than one-tenth of Members are, the man of whose life Parliament is only a part, the juryman with no desire whatever to sit on the bench; whose verdict is for that very reason the more important and respected; whose loss is deeply to be deplored and may prove fatal to Parliament itself.' Since the abolition of the university seats in 1950 a Member of Parliament has had in practice to belong to a political party. He has had to be personally and politically acceptable to a small clique of persons who run the political organization in his constituency and to the central organization of his party. He is expected to accept the discipline of his parliamentary party and the test of his loyalty is often his willingness to support his leaders, even when he believes them to be wrong. Unlike the American Senate or Congress, membership of the House of Commons is not normally thought to constitute a career in itself. The Prime Minister of the day has patronage to dispense in the form of office which can embrace about a hundred of the members of the majority party in the House of Commons. Conservative Prime Ministers often generously reward their loyal parliamentary supporters with knighthoods. An MP's term can be abruptly terminated at two weeks' notice (as mine was), not because of anything that he has done or has not done, but at the whim of the reigning Prime Minister. Until recently Labour Members of Parliament were bound by the standing orders of the Parliamentary Labour Party. During my time in Parliament five Labour Members had the Whip withdrawn for abstaining in a parliamentary division. It is small wonder if the Member of Parliament feels that there are considerable pressures on him to conform.

Not only is the Member of Parliament of all parties bound by the rigid discipline which I have described, but he is frustrated in other ways. He seldom has access to information which is not available to the general public. Government Policy is frequently announced to Parliament, or even through the Press, without his fore-knowledge. He has very little opportunity to influence policy or even to make his views known before decisions have been taken which he is expected to support by his vote and voice in subsequent parliamentary debates, as indeed was the case with the Government's emergency economic measures of July, 1966.

If an MP disagrees with his party on an issue he is liable to be attacked from two quarters, the Whips at Westminster and his constituency association. The pattern of discipline varies in the two main parties. A right wing revolt in the Conservative Party and a left wing revolt in the Labour Party are usually tolerated and sometimes even encouraged in the constituencies. The sanction of removing the Whip has been frequently used in the Parliamentary Labour Party but is hardly known in the Conservative Party. However, the effect of removing the parliamentary Whip from a Labour Member can be exaggerated since it has almost invariably been restored well in advance of a General Election, thus allowing the victim to fight under his party's banner when party support is most needed. A stricter sanction which is more rarely employed is expulsion from the Labour Party, from which a return to grace is more difficult, although not unknown. The fact that such important figures in the Labour movement as Sir Stafford Cripps, Aneurin Bevan (twice), Sidney Silverman and Michael Foot have suffered under one or both of these processes, and that Cripps and Bevan subsequently served in Labour Cabinets, and Bevan four years after the Whip was withdrawn for the second time actually became the Deputy Leader of the Labour Party, suggests that Labour parliamentary discipline is unrealistic and unnecessarily harsh. The signs are that it is being ameliorated under the present Crossman/Silkin regime.

While Conservative parliamentary discipline is ostensibly more civilized (I voted against my party six times between 1959 and 1966 without being threatened with the removal of the Whip), constituency pressures are immeasurably greater. I have observed that right wing revolts are usually forgiven by Conservative constituency associations. Thus no action was taken at constituency level against those Members of Parliament who fought the Government on self-rule for India in the 1930s or even against those who refused the Conservative Whip in 1957 in protest against the withdrawal from Suez after the failure of Eden's intervention. Quite different standards, however, apply to what are regarded as left wing revolts on foreign policy issues and still more to left wing stands on those matters of social reform which seem to inflame Conservative constituency associations, such as the abolition of hanging and of judicial corporal punishment and homosexual law reform. There is also a general feeling inside local Conservative associations that if their Member does not support the party leadership, he is in some way being disloyal. Sir Winston Churchill fought his constituency association and the Whips and the Conservative Central Office before the war and would almost certainly not have been adopted as an official candidate in the anticipated General Election of 1939 for the party which he was to lead only a year later. Though not in any sense a left wing politician, the fact that he had made common cause with the Liberals and the bulk of the Labour party in opposition to the Munich Agreement was not forgiven until the war which he sought to avert had started.

Of those Members of Parliament who protested against the Suez intervention Mr Anthony Nutting, who resigned as Minister of State at the Foreign Office, was forced to resign from his seat at Melton Mowbray; Sir Frank Medlicott was not readopted at Central Norfolk; and Mr Nigel Nicolson, after a prolonged battle, was refused renomination by his constituency association at Bournemouth (contrary to the wishes of the Conservative Central Office), since in addition to his views on Suez he was also an opponent of capital punishment. When Mr Iain Macleod, a former Chairman of the Conservative Party, refused to serve in Sir Alec Douglas-Home's Cabinet in 1963, there were open moves in his constituency to have him replaced by a more amenable candidate, though less than two years later he was to become the Conservative Party's chief spokesman on economic affairs.

I first voted against my party in 1961 in support of the re-nunciation of peerages, which stemmed from the wish of Mr Wedgwood Benn to remain in the House of Commons after the death of his father the 1st Viscount Stansgate. I was strongly censured by the Conservative Whips, but supported by my constituency officers. I was afterwards forgiven for a rebellion in which, as it happens, Sir Alec Douglas-Home proved sub-sequently to have been the principal beneficiary. I was, however, in continual difficulties with members of my association over my stand in favour of independence for African dependent territories. One of my branch officers resigned after I had become the first Conservative Member of Parliament to advocate the release of

Jomo Kenyatta from restriction. Many of the Conservative voters of Lancaster subsequently became ardent supporters of the Smith rebellion in Rhodesia. I encountered trouble both from the Whips and from members of my Association when I abstained at the end of the Profumo debate in 1963, and again when later that year I strongly attacked the method by which Sir Alec Douglas-Home had become Prime Minister and leader of the Conservative Party. Again I was in part forgiven when the Conservative Party adopted a method which I had advocated for choosing its new leader.

I encountered no hostility from the Conservative Whips—quite the reverse—when I became a sponsor of Mr Sidney Silverman's Bill to abolish capital punishment and when, having drawn second place in the Private Members' ballot, I decided to introduce a measure to reform the law relating to homosexual practices committed between consenting male adults in private. At this point, however, I ran into serious difficulties with members of my local Conservative association. There were open moves, which were ultimately defeated, to have me replaced by another candidate for the General Election which took place in March 1966. The officers of one ward, the safest as it happens from the Conservative point of view, refused to work on my behalf, and it is estimated that approximately a thousand Conservatives abstained from voting because of my sponsorship of the Sexual Offences Bill. I shall always be grateful to the officers of the Lancaster Conservative Association for their personal loyalty to me when they disagreed with so much that I did.

If it is agreed that our form of parliamentary government is breaking down because the executive has seized unbridled power from the legislature, there are two immediate needs. They are separate but interrelated. Firstly, Parliament must be given the means to scrutinize policy. Secondly, Members of Parliament must be given a secure tenure which is neither dependent on the pleasure of the executive nor solely reliant upon the favour of the local party caucus.

The proposal to set up specialist committees, which I have already discussed, would go a long way towards meeting the first requirement. Rules of procedure should be altered to enable Parliament at will to debate matters of immediate concern. The televising of Parliament, which is merely the logical extension of the decision in the eighteenth century to admit the press into Parliamentary proceedings, would also help to repatriate political issues from the studios to Westminster where they properly belong. Admirable though these reforms in themselves might be, they are ancillary to the main problem—the status, security and independence of Members of Parliament.

In practice, a parliamentary candidate, once endorsed by his party's central organization, is chosen by a small body of at most a hundred local party supporters. If the seat is safe he is elected; if it is marginal his election depends upon a favourable political climate. The local caucus may be quite remote from the mass of party voters in the constituency. Yet his fate is in their hands. He could most easily be freed from this bondage by a system of 'primary elections', adapted from the American pattern, in which the field of choice was extended beyond the narrow range of committed party workers to all supporters within the constituency of the party whose candidate he aspires to become. This innovation would have the double virtue of associating more closely the supporters of a particular party with the candidate for whom they will be asked to cast their vote and of giving to the candidate or Member a body fully representative of his support in his constituency, to whom he could appeal in the event of his falling out with his local committee or the Whips at Westminster.

A further reform which I advocate is the introduction of the alternative vote in parliamentary elections. Under this system, which would preserve the single member constituency, if the leading candidate does not obtain an overall majority of votes, those votes cast for the candidate who comes bottom of the poll are redistributed according to a second preference which is indicated when the original vote is cast. If necessary, successive candidates at the bottom of the poll are eliminated until one candidate receives an overall majority. The advantages of this particular electoral reform are threefold. Firstly, there is no such phenomenon as a wasted vote since an elector who chooses to cast his first vote in favour of a Liberal, Communist, Nationalist or an Independent candidate is not deprived of indicating his preference for a candidate belonging to one of the two main parties. Secondly, a Labour or Conservative Member who had quarrelled with his local committee or with the Whips could stand as an Independent and appeal for support from the rank and file of his own party without the fear of letting in the other side. Thirdly, at least on second preferences, cross-party voting would be encouraged and thus a genuine vote for the man rather than the party might emerge.

The two reforms which I have suggested would undoubtedly strengthen the position of the Member of Parliament locally while broadening the base of his potential support. As such they would go some way towards increasing his independence and status. There remains a fundamental weakness in his position as a Member of the legislature. In the United States the Executive cannot dismiss Congress and Congress cannot dismiss the Executive. In Britain the Executive, or to be more pointed the Prime Minister, can at any moment dismiss Parliament. In theory of course Parliament through a vote of censure can obtain the resignation of the Government, but the pressures are such that except in times of war, when party considerations might no longer apply, this is inconceivable.

The post-war years have shown that the power of dissolution is the most potent and dangerous weapon which the executive possesses; it enables the Prime Minister to go to the country at a time best suited to him and his party and, by a careful adjustment of policies, it makes the Government of the day almost impossible to overthrow. It has gone a long way towards reducing Members of Parliament into cyphers. It must therefore be removed.

There are two alternative methods of giving Members of Parliament a measure of security of tenure in their seats. In the first place it would be possible to have a fixed five-year Parliament. This would have presented no difficulties in five out of the seven post-war Parliaments. Had the Parliaments of 1950 and 1964 run their full course, five years of deadlock might have ensued. However as it happened, in each case a Labour Government was capable of governing effectively for a period of eighteen months and could possibly have done so, perhaps at the price of delaying more controversial pieces of legislation, for a full Parliament. It might in any event be thought constitutionally proper, in the absence of an effective delaying power on the part of the House of Lords, for a Government to be curbed from pursuing extreme policies owing to the narrowness of its Parliamentary majority and in the absence of a more emphatic endorsement of its programme by the electorate.

An alternative reform would be for Members of Parliament to be given a fixed six-year term with, say, a third of the six hundred Members retiring every two years. Under such a system General Elections would no longer take place. The most obvious disadvantage of this proposal would be the danger of electioneering every two years. However, even under our present system Parliament lived in an atmosphere of continual electioneering from the summer of 1963 until the spring of 1966, during which period the House of Commons could at any time have been dissolved at a few weeks' notice. Unattractive as bi-annual electioneering may seem, it is perhaps preferable to the post-war practice of Governments of both parties spending the first two years of each Parliament pushing through unpopular measures so that the economy can be manipulated into a favourable state ready for a General Election at a time of the Government's choosing. A bi-annual election of a third of Parliament would also avoid the massive Parliamentary majorities of 1945, 1959 and 1966 with the tendency to arrogance on the part of the governing party which they encouraged.

The Member of Parliament at the beginning of this century owed much of his security to his financial independence. He had to be a man of means, because not only were Members not paid a parliamentary salary but they were also responsible for meeting their own election expenses and for paying the cost of running their local party machines. Until 1948 many Conservative safe seats were quite shamelessly auctioned to the highest bidder. After the Second World War a Conservative Party committee, under the chairmanship of Sir David Maxwell Fyffe, rightly recommended that no Conservative candidate or Member should be allowed to make large contributions to local party funds, thus ensuring that merit rather than wealth should be the criterion for selection. This forced local Conservative associations to be financially independent of their Members. Ironically it also lessened the independence of the Member, who could then more easily be got rid of, once he ceased to finance the local machine.

The payment of a comparatively large salary of £3,250 a year to Members of Parliament has in other ways had the effect of reducing a Member's independence. For, while it has eliminated humiliating poverty from the experience of the Member, the salary is sufficiently attractive for many potential Parliamentary candidates to regard a career in Westminster as actually financially rewarding. The temptation of the Member without other means of financial support to toe the Party line is correspondingly increased.

I do not in the least deplore these developments (indeed there is a strong case for paying in addition for MPs to have individual secretarial and research staff) but they have created a need to provide safeguards for the Member's independence and integrity, such as I have described. Most of them already exist in the United States where the Congressman or Senator is far more amply rewarded for his services.

No one who has spent any length of time in the House of Commons would wish the legislature to usurp the role of the executive. Congress has never attempted to do this. Nevertheless it ought to be possible for a Member of Parliament of the Government party to take as critical a line of Government policy as that taken by Senator Kennedy over Vietnam and still survive. Churchill was able to do this in the pre-war years—to the lasting benefit of the nation. I doubt if it would be possible today.

CHAPTER VIII

THE HOUSE OF LORDS

At least three constitutional myths surround the House of Lords. The first is that there is still a meaningful clash between the Lords and Commons in terms of powers. The second is that the institution of life peerages has transformed what would otherwise be a reactionary and even bloodthirsty chamber of hereditary backwoodsmen into an enlightened and progressive assembly. And the third is that the role played by the House of Lords as a revising chamber is so essential that if there were no Upper House in Britain one would have to be invented.

In 1934 the Labour Party Conference passed a resolution that 'A Labour Government meeting with sabotage from the House of Lords would take immediate steps to overcome it; and it will in any event take steps during its term of office to pass legislation abolishing the House of Lords as a legislative chamber'. The Labour Party Manifesto of 1935 contained a clause to abolish the House of Lords. However, Herbert Morrison in *Government and Parliament* admitted that 'during the Labour Governments of 1945–1951, they treated us with consideration as indeed was our due'. The pledge to abolish the House of Lords has been tacitly forgotten. The Parliament Act of 1949 under the post-war Labour Government reduced the delaying power of the House of Lords from two years to one year; this was presumably in conformity with the pledge that the Labour Party had given in its election manifesto 'Let us Face the Future', in which it said 'We give clear notice that we will not tolerate obstruction of the people's will by the House of Lords'.

The Parliament Act of 1911 first gave the Commons the power to insist on certain Bills being passed into law without the assent of the Lords. In fact only three bills have become law under the Parliament Act of 1911—the Government of Ireland Bill (1914), the Welsh Disestablishment Bill (1914), and the Parliament Bill (1949). A fourth bill, the Iron and Steel Bill (1949), was voluntarily delayed by the Labour Government as part of a bargain with the House of Lords. The operation of this bill was deferred in a Lords amendment until after the latest possible date for the next General Election, by which time the electorate would have had a chance to decide on the merits of steel nationalization for itself. No bill has become law under the Parliament Act (1949), and Lord Carrington, the leader of the Conservative Party in the House of Lords, has expressed the view that the House of Lords could not reject a major Government measure and survive with its present powers.[1] It is clear that the ancient battle over power has ended, though the main victor has been the executive rather than the House of Commons.[2]

It is often quite inaccurately supposed that apart from the delaying power nothing has been done to implement the preamble to the Parliament Act of 1911, which heralded drastic reform of the Second Chamber. It is true that the composition of the House of Lords was not altered for forty-seven years and that even now the Second Chamber is not constituted on a popular basis as the Act forecast. Nevertheless, the present House of Lords is essentially the creation of the Conservative Government of Mr Harold Macmillan, as between 1957 and 1963 four measures were introduced which transformed the nature of the Second Chamber.

First, the payment of expenses for peers was authorised in 1957; this originally amounted to three guineas a day and was raised to four and a half guineas a day in 1965. Secondly, under a

---

[1] The House of Lords, February 16, 1967.

[2] I regard the Government proposal still further to reduce the powers of the House of Lords as announced on October 31, 1967, in the Queen's Speech as unnecessary and irrelevant.

standing order of May 24, 1958, a procedure was introduced (of which some 200 peers have taken advantage) allowing peers to apply for leave of absence either for the forthcoming session or for the whole of the forthcoming Parliament. This has effectively reduced the size of the House of Lords by two hundred 'back-woodsmen'. Much more important was the Life Peerages Act of 1958: by October 1, 1967, life peers consisted of 154 out of a maximum working peerage of about 700. The hereditary principle which many people found the most objectionable feature of an unreformed House of Lords having thus been breached, it was logical to provide for the renunciation of peerages on the part of those who succeeded to peerages and who wished to remain commoners. This was provided, after a two-year struggle by Mr Anthony Wedgwood Benn, supported by a number of Conservatives (including myself), in the Peerage Act of 1963.

Although the Life Peerages Act has undoubtedly strengthened the House of Lords, the Peerage Act (allowing for renunciation) can hardly be said to have greatly weakened it—even though it provided the vehicle for the return to the Commons of Sir Alec Douglas-Home, Mr Quintin Hogg and Mr Wedgwood Benn. While the Life Peerages Act has gone some way to redressing the party balance in the House of Lords (the latest figures of those taking party whips being Conservative 300, Labour 91, and Liberal 43) it has not made it a more noticeably progressive chamber than it would anyway have been. For counting the votes of hereditary peers only in second readings of the Sexual Offences Bill, the abolition of capital punishment and in the debate on Rhodesia Oil Sanctions—between 1965 and 1966—72 against 41 voted in favour of homosexual law reform, 141 against 99 voted in favour of the abolition of the death penalty and 59 against 19 voted in favour of oil sanctions against Rhodesia.

In a straight vote on a major party political issue, including the votes of both life and hereditary peers, the Government was defeated by 107 votes to 55 on the defence estimates in March 1966. Given the fact that Mr Wilson recommended the creation of 75 life peerages between October 1964 and August 1967 it is clear that the automatic Conservative majority on the few occasions when votes of this kind take place could soon be eliminated, even without eliminating the hereditary peers.

The role of the House of Lords as a revising chamber has startlingly diminished since the immediate post-war years. During the 1945/1951 Labour Governments many bills were guillotined by the House of Commons and consequently needed revision by the House of Lords. In the ten major bills of 1946/1947 the Lords made 1,222 amendments of which only 57 were rejected by the Commons. In the session 1964/1965 the number of amendments passed by the House of Lords to House of Commons bills had dwindled to about 130, many of them being of a purely formal or drafting character. Government amendments proper, to quote Mr J. R. Vincent in the autumn 1966 issue of Parliamentary Affairs, which were almost invariably passed without a division 'are not the work of lynx-eyed elder statesmen ruthlessly scrutinizing the work of the parliamentary draughtsmen. They are the work of the draughtsmen and officials, dotting the i's and crossing the t's of their work with rare pedantry and refinement.'

Sir Ivor Jennings, in Government and Parliament, saw a role for the House of Lords beyond that of legislating. Pointing out that the Commons is mostly concerned with Government legislation he went on to say, 'There is neither time nor opportunity (for the House of Commons) to discuss some of the broader issues of policy such as those which relate to foreign affairs, defence, colonies, and commonwealth relations which do not require immediate legislation and are not in party controversy'. But these are exactly the topics which should be under scrutiny from parliamentary select committees, and although the House of Lords fulfils a useful function in debating these subjects from time to time in default of an airing elsewhere this should not be left to the Upper House alone. It should indeed be the interest primarily of the Lower House which after all is the chamber largely responsible for questioning Ministers on the conduct of their departments.

It is perhaps appropriate to examine Second Chamber constitutions employed by other countries. The British and American Second Chambers are both unique. The House of Lords is the only Upper House to contain a (predominately) hereditary element;[1] the United States senate is the only Upper House more powerful than the Lower. In Canada the senate consists of 102 members who are appointed for life by the Governor-General of Canada on the advice of the Prime Minister. In effect Canadian senators are life peers, though the Prime Minister's power of nomination is limited to filling existing vacancies. The powers of the Canadian senate are in theory equal to those of the elected chamber except on money bills. In Ireland and Norway at the beginning of each new session the elected Members of Parliament select from among their number a fixed proportion (one third in Ireland and a quarter in Norway) to form a body with wide powers which is a cross between an Upper Chamber and a glorified committee. In Sweden members of the Upper Chamber are nominated by local councils. Co-operation between the chambers is ensured by constitutional law. All bills must be considered by joint committees of both Houses before being voted upon individually by each. If the two Houses differ on a money bill, it must be discussed and voted upon in a joint session of both Houses, all members (there are 150 in the Upper House and 230 in the Lower House) carrying equal weight and equal votes.

The Second Chamber in France has changed too frequently for study to be profitable. In New Zealand between 1891 and 1951 the 40 members of the Upper House were appointed for seven years by the Governor-General on the Prime Minister's advice. Appointments were made purely on party lines and the Second Chamber was abolished in 1951.

At this stage we should consider the purpose of a Second Chamber within the framework of the British Parliamentary

---

[1] This will presumably be altered under the plans for House of Lords Reform announced in the Queen's Speech on October 31, 1967.

System. A Second Chamber 'constituted on a popular instead of hereditary basis', to quote the words of the 1911 Parliament Act, would presumably be elected in some form. In this event a degree of rivalry between two elected chambers would be inevitable. If the Second Chamber was elected for the same period as the Lower House it would reflect the same party strengths, unless proportional representation were used for the electoral process in one chamber and not in the other. If the Second Chamber were elected for a longer or shorter term than the Lower House the same sterile argument over respective powers would break out again. There is no parallel with the United States where the Senate protects the smaller states in a Federal constitution. I believe, therefore, that the House of Lords should not be an elected body and following from that assumption that it is not intended to compete with the Commons and that its legislative powers should not, therefore, be greatly altered.

The House of Lords in its present form strengthens the institution of Parliament in three ways. First, owing to the growth of the party machines it is the only parliamentary vehicle for the independent unwhipped expression of opinion. It is quite unrealistic to imagine that since the abolition of the university seats independents will ever be elected to the House of Commons again.[1] Secondly, as the House of Commons becomes more demanding upon the time of Members of Parliament, it must be to the House of Lords that one must look for the representatives of the active leaders of Industry and the Trades Unions if these are to play any role in the legislative life of the country at all. Thirdly, as we have seen in recent years with the introduction in the first instance of both the Abortion Law Reform Bill and the Homosexual Law Reform Bill in the House of Lords, the Upper House can play an indispensable part in the introduction to Parliament of Private Members' Bills. In February 1966 I intro-

---

[1] The Nationalist candidates in Scotland and Wales who have been returned in by-elections are not Independents but represent a genuine grievance on the part of Scottish and Welsh electors.

duced the Sexual Offences Bill in the House of Commons, where it obtained a second reading by a substantial majority. This measure was killed when Parliament was dissolved four weeks later. The fact, however, that the Bill had originally been introduced into the House of Lords by Lord Arran and had been through all its stages before it came to the Commons undoubtedly influenced the Government in its decision to give it Government time in the House of Commons. The Government decided on this when it was re-introduced by Mr Leo Abse after the General Election under the ten-minute rule procedure, despite the fact that he had not (as I had) obtained a place in the ballot for private members' time.

The fact that the House of Lords contains a hereditary element at all is undoubtedly an anachronism which, so long as it persists, makes many people reluctant to take it seriously as a legislative body. In the view of Sir Ivor Jennings 'Clearly the simplest solution is to separate the right to a writ of summons from a hereditary peerage' (i.e. the right to attend). This proposal, though in my view right, is not as radical as it may sound. For although the number of life peers is still only a hundred and fifty four out of a maximum working membership in the House of Lords of over seven hundred, the number of hereditary peers of first creation (as opposed to peers by succession) is a hundred and forty and these should clearly be regarded as Lords of Parliament for life (who could have anyway been created Life Peers) for the purposes of this calculation. In addition there are, of course, twenty-six bishops with a right to a seat in the House of Lords. If hereditary peers by succession, therefore, were excluded from membership of the House of Lords we would be left with an Upper House which already numbers more than three hundred. In such a body it would clearly be right to include the leaders of religious bodies other than the Church of England. I would also support the creation of Lords of Parliament for a fixed term of,[1] say, six years.

---

[1] In addition to life peers.

This would allow Members of Parliament who had been defeated at a General Election to play a parliamentary role without denying themselves the opportunity of ultimately returning to the House of Commons; it would also enable a person to accept a temporary peerage without the irrevocability of the choice which is now presented to him. A further reform of parliamentary procedure which I consider to be long overdue would allow Ministers to speak and answer questions (but not vote) in either House of Parliament. This would remove any constitutional difficulty in the way of a Peer holding any Cabinet office, excluding that of Chancellor of the Exchequer.

I have suggested the ways in which the House of Lords can be of value as a Legislative Chamber and also how it could most sensibly be constituted. I also believe that it has a role to play in the restoration of power to the legislature thus curbing the power of the executive. I have discussed the role of parliamentary specialist committees in an earlier chapter. I believe that the House of Lords should participate in these and that each such committee should be a joint committee of both Houses. I envisage that the House of Commons would have a majority on each committee. This would produce a substantial streamlining of parliamentary business, as each measure after its second reading in each House would then go through a joint committee stage of both Houses and it would only have to go back to the individual chambers for report and third reading. Under this procedure the supremacy of the House of Commons would not be challenged, both because it would have a majority on the specialist committee and also because at the report stage it would be able to reverse committee amendments if this was thought desirable.

From these proposals it is clear that a substantial number of 'working peers' will be needed in order to man the specialist committees. I therefore envisage payment for peers comparable to that of Members of Parliament.

Writing a hundred years ago, Bagehot was in favour both of House of Lords reform and also the creation of life peers. 'The danger of the House of Commons is perhaps that it will be reformed too rashly; the danger of the House of Lords certainly is that it may never be reformed.' As we have seen in the case of the House of Lords this has not proved to be true, but reform has been piecemeal and until the last ten years concerned only with its powers relative to those of the House of Commons. In the last ten years thought has been given to its composition and to some degree changes have been implemented. It is now necessary to create the conditions in which the House of Lords in co-operation with the House of Commons becomes one of the checks which makes the Presidential rule of the Prime Minister tolerable. For this reason I support the total elimination of the hereditary element in the House of Lords but I oppose any attempt to reduce the powers of a reconstituted chamber.

CHAPTER IX

CONCLUSIONS

The people of Britain have noted with regret, although not without a trace of complacency, that the Westminster pattern of parliamentary government has failed to last more than a few experimental years in most new Commonwealth countries. What the British have not, for the most part, recognized is that parliamentary democracy has now collapsed at Westminster. Just as the existence of the Commonwealth and the adherence to it of each newly independent colony disguised from the colonels of Cheltenham the unprecedentedly rapid liquidation of Empire until protest was too late to be effective, so there seems to be something tantamount to a conspiracy (to which both television and newspapers are party) to disguise the decline of parliamentary control at Westminster. Headlines such as 'Uproar at Question Time' or 'Wilson flays Heath' and radio announcements such as 'The House of Commons had another all-night sitting last night' combine to convey the impression that Westminster is a place where matters of real importance to the nation still take place. This misconception has an exact similarity with the so-called Anglo-American special relationship. It represents a myth which is no longer valid.

I have argued that the basic defect in the British system of Government is the supra-presidential power of the Prime Minister. I am willing to concede him quasi-presidential authority and I have suggested ways in which his domestic power might be reduced to this level.

The principal need is to remove from the Prime Minister the power to dissolve Parliament, by giving the legislature a fixed term of life independent of the executive. There remains the problem which I have described in Chapter V of disposing of an unpopular or senile Prime Minister without recourse to what Richard Crossman has termed 'a coup-d'état'.

It is difficult enough to dispose of a party leader who is not a Prime Minister. The Labour leader goes through a process of annual re-election; but since Lord Attlee survived this ritual for twenty successive years without challenge, it would not be unfair to describe the process as being often something of a formality. Nevertheless the fact that Hugh Gaitskell, while surviving as Labour leader until his death, was openly challenged after he first became leader by both Anthony Greenwood and Wilson in a public contest with a published voting result shows that there exists a means of removing a Labour leader who has lost the confidence of the party, while the party is in opposition.

In the Conservative Party no such mechanism exists. In the winter of 1964 I submitted a memorandum to Sir Alec Douglas-Home, then Leader of the Conservative Party, which contained proposals as to how future Conservative Leaders should be elected. I argued that there ought to be a secret ballot confined to Members of Parliament who would vote for openly competing candidates for the position of leader of the Parliamentary Party in the knowledge that the results of their voting would be published. I also recommended that the traditional Party meeting consisting of peers, Members of Parliament, parliamentary candidates and members of the National Union Executive Committee should be retained to confirm the Parliamentary leader as leader of the party as a whole. These suggestions were incorporated in the system which Sir Alec finally presented to the Conservative Party, together with a highly complicated device (which I had not recommended) requiring the victor to obtain not only an overall majority of votes, but a lead of 15 per cent over his nearest rival. This device was not clearly understood at the time; it did not operate at the time of Mr Heath's election since, owing to his bare overall majority, his opponents withdrew; it is unlikely to be heard of again.

My memorandum to Sir Alec contained one recommendation which was not in fact accepted, namely that the Conservative Party leader should be elected at the beginning of each Parliament. The Conservative Party, indeed any party, might not wish to continue to be led by a leader who had lost two elections in succession. In fact, in this century only two party leaders apart from Churchill of the major parties have survived two successive defeats—Balfour and Attlee. Both had the additional prestige of being former Prime Ministers. Attlee voluntarily retired a few months later in 1955, and Balfour was forced to resign in 1911 only after an internal and protracted squabble of the type which I was trying to avoid. I hope that the Conservative Party will in time come to recognize the merit of my proposal. This would, however, merely be a variation on the Labour system and could only be effective in solving the internal problems of a party in defeat.

Once a party leader becomes Prime Minister, and so long as he is Prime Minister, he is in practice only removable if he is too ill to remain in office or if there is a war. It is no coincidence that Churchill, Eden and Macmillan were forced out of office by illness and that all of them remained as Prime Ministers for some-time after their physical powers had begun to wane. In the circumstances and to mitigate, though not of course to avoid this danger, I would be in favour of limiting a Prime Minister's tenure of office to two fixed terms of Parliament or a maximum of eight years. Paradoxically this limitation would not have affected any of the three Prime Ministers whom I have mentioned, as the tendency has been for elderly men to become Prime Ministers. However, if we are now in a period, as seems likely, of younger party leaders, this limitation might be wise.

Because I believe that there should be a parallel process of curbing the power of the Prime Minister and increasing the power of Parliament, I have recommended three proposals to strengthen the power of the backbencher: a system of primaries; election to Parliament through the alternative vote system; and a considerable extension of the number, powers and scope of parliamentary committees. The case for these particular reforms has already been fully argued.

The chief problem is how to bring about reforms of this sweeping nature. I cannot escape the feeling that the Conservative Party as a whole, while deploring the fact that Mr Wilson enjoys the powers that he does, takes the view that this unsatisfactory position would somehow be corrected by a change to a Tory Prime Minister. It is central to my argument that the power of the Prime Minister is altogether too great, regardless of who occupies No. 10 Downing Street.

At the Conservative Party Conference held at Blackpool in 1966, Mr Heath spoke about 'the Great Divide'. I do not criticize him for so doing, since it is the duty of the leader of the Opposition to outline the alternatives that his party can offer.

However, at a time when both British political parties are committed to Britain's entry into Europe, when Mr Heath has accepted the comprehensive ideal for secondary education, and when the Labour Party is moving in the direction of a policy of selectivity for the social services, the 'great divide' is not the most obvious hall-mark of the British political system.

There have been in British politics issues of such profound importance that they have not only divided public opinion; they have also broken down the monolithic unity of the parties themselves. The protracted and agonizing debate over Home Rule for Ireland was one such issue, and the pre-war issue of re-armament and anti-appeasement was another. I believe that the question of Parliamentary Reform comes within this category. Many people, possibly a majority, are disillusioned with politics and with our parliamentary institutions. They instinctively feel that something is wrong, even if they cannot define what it is. This book is an attempt to define the nature of the problem and to suggest some remedies. It is my belief that the political party which adopts the cause of parliamentary reform will gain, and deserve, massive support from the country as a whole.

INDEX

For Product Safety Concerns and Information please contact our EU
representative GPSR@taylorandfrancis.com
Taylor & Francis Verlag GmbH, Kaufingerstraße 24, 80331 München, Germany